# Unfolded Hands

⎫
⎬
⎭

Aidan Rogers

All quoted Scripture and Bible references are taken from the God's Word translation unless otherwise noted.

Copyright © 2013 Aidan Rogers
All rights reserved.
ISBN: 149215498
ISBN-13: 978-1492152491

To the women who have taught me what it means to be strong, to give generously, to live graciously, and to love well: Tina, Dottie, Becky, and Inez

# CONTENTS

| | |
|---|---|
| *Preface: How Then Should I Pray* | *iii* |
| *The Power of Prayer* | *1* |
| *Superstition* | *9* |
| *Honest Prayer* | *19* |
| *Demand Fullness* | *27* |
| *Straight Up Pray* | *37* |
| *The Implausible Dream* | *47* |
| *Pray Today* | *53* |
| *Pray Out Loud* | *61* |
| *Pray Drunk* | *69* |
| *Pray Continually* | *77* |
| *Paradoxology* | *85* |
| *Pray Unconditionally* | *93* |
| *Thy Will Be Done* | *103* |
| *Come* | *111* |
| *Healed* | *119* |
| *Pray For Me* | *127* |
| *Do Not Be Afraid* | *135* |
| *Holy Moments* | *143* |
| *Holy Words* | *151* |
| *Why* | *159* |
| *Strangely Warm* | *167* |
| *In the Name of Jesus* | *175* |
| *Amen* | *183* |
| *Afterword: A New Way Home* | *191* |

## ACKNOWLEDGMENTS

Special thanks to Diane for faithfully reading as many drafts as I could walk across the street. Your feedback has been invaluable in making this book what it is.

Thanks to the handful of others who have read chapters here and there.

Thanks to the elders, ministers, brothers and sisters who have taught me how to pray. And encouraged me to pray, even when I was certain I was doing it wrong or not enough or maybe too often.

And thanks to the Father who hears me when I pray, no matter how messed up, backward, or awkward my words sometimes come out. I know that You hear me, and I am honored and humbled to hear back from You.

# \ Preface: How Then Should I Pray /

Prayer is arguably one of the most difficult disciplines of the Christian life. When I was in youth group, we used to joke that the answer to any question was, "Pray, read the Bible, go to church." Read the Bible is easy – I either do or I don't. Go to church is the same, either I'm there or I'm not. But what exactly does it mean to pray?

It is a tough question. We are told prayer is this or prayer is that, that it is about getting the right words or the right posture or the right presentation. It is about folding our hands and bowing our heads and using holy-sounding words to beseech (a holy-sounding word in itself) our God. I don't find this definition particularly helpful. It doesn't look like anything I see in the Bible.

The prayer I see in the Bible is powerful. It is beyond powerful; it is amazing. The way these men and women prayed and God responded...that is how I want to pray. I want to pray the kind of honest, raw prayer that hide nothing from my God. I want to pray the kind of prayer that makes my wretched, wrecked heart seem like the most beautiful offering in all of creation.

I've never done it with all the ritual we pray today. I have never gotten there with my head bowed and eyes shut. I have never prayed the kind of prayer I long to pray with folded hands.

That's one of the troubles with the way we pray. We have ritualized prayer to all but eliminate the relationship, so that prayer is an exercise in structure and form rather than faith and love.

We have rules for praying, guidelines to follow. We fold our hands to keep from twiddling our thumbs. We bow our heads to keep our minds from wandering. And we close our eyes so we are not drawn away from this sanctified, holy moment. We start with a *Dear Lord*, much like writing a form letter, and muddle through the middle with a jumbled mess of holy-sounding words, weaving in a perfect balance of praise and petition, thanksgiving and angst, goodwill and grief until we get to an *amen*.

We burden ourselves with getting prayer "right." There is a right way to pray, a good and God-honoring way, which we have formalized. Anything else is a lesser prayer, an offense to God, and quite obviously "wrong."

This makes prayer a heavy burden. We pray and we pray and we pray again, and when we have finished praying, we pray some more because this empty place inside of us tells us that we can pray better. A lot better.

We must pray better because our prayers have gone unanswered. It seems God has not heard. That has to be our fault, we decide. We missed a step here or there. We opened our eyes, raised our head, unfolded our hands a millisecond too early. We weren't fully focused on praying the prayer. We did too much griping and not enough giving, too much petition without enough praise. We forgot to say, "In the name of Jesus" or dare we admit? We forgot the "amen." We analyze our prayer to death over the ritual and agonize over praying better, all while coming to one devastating conclusion:

This isn't working. It's not working for me.

Another problem with the way we pray is we consider our words "a" prayer, as though prayer is a thing to be done or performed or perfected.

Prayer is not a thing. We never have a prayer the same way we have a television or a comfy chair or a candy bar. Yet this is our vernacular. This is the way we say it. We hold hands around the dinner table and ask our family to say "a" prayer. We invite an elder to stand before the congregation and offer "a" prayer. We kneel with our children at night and teach them to say "a" prayer before climbing into bed. Together, we say "our" prayers.

When "a" prayer is "a" thing, it takes all of the action out of it. We start throwing around prayers like we're giving away dollars. It's just a thing. It's just an item. It's something we give.

But prayer is not a gift; it's an offering. It is not something we hand out; it is something we pour out.

Prayer is something we do; it is a discipline. It requires the full engagement of the body, the spirit, the heart, and the soul. It demands the investment of our whole presence into one tiny holy moment. It takes everything we have to pray one honest word because it is not merely words; prayer is an encounter.

It is an encounter with the living God who takes your folded hands in His. It is an encounter with the incredible God who raises your head to see His glory. It is an encounter with the awesome God who opens your eyes to see His face. Prayer is an encounter with the God who stands before you.

*pray*

And I think it's better to stand before Him with open hands. That's what I think about when I think about powerful prayer.

An open hand is able to touch the God who stands before you. An open hand knows what His presence feels like. Think about the woman with chronic bleeding who touched the robe of Christ as He walked by. Do you imagine her hands were folded in His presence? Was it a holy fist-bump of the tunic so she could both seek her God and honor Him with ritual at the same time?

I doubt it. She touched Him with an open hand, and He healed her.

An open hand gives good gifts to God; it presents an offering. The Old Testament priests were instructed in the ritual of sacrifice. They were told to take this or that piece of the slaughtered animal, hold it high to the heavens, and pronounce a blessing in the name of God. Do you think they did this with folded hands? Were they balancing a ram's hock on bended knuckles, cautiously raising it before the Lord?

Hardly. They were holding the offering high with open hands, holy and pleasing to the Lord.

An open hand receives good gifts from God. In the Upper Room, Jesus breaks the bread and starts handing it out to the disciples. Do you think they took it with folded hands? Did Jesus tuck a few crumbs in the creases of their palms as they shared a holy meal together?

Of course not. He gave them the bread and with open hands, they took it and ate.

An open hand holds out hope. In Mark 8, Jesus takes the hand of a blind man and leads him away to a private place, where He heals the man.

An open hand carries praise. How often do you see a man in worship raise a fist to the Lord? Never. You raise a hand.

No one comes into God's presence with folded hands. He never asks them to. He is always giving, taking, touching, holding, hoping, honoring, and loving. We are always longing to give, take, touch, hold, hope, honor, and love. We can't do these things with folded hands.

# Preface

It isn't working.

*pray*

We know it isn't working because we pray and don't feel like we've come into the presence of God. Yet that is all that prayer is – being in a place to talk with Him, walk with Him, lean on Him, listen to Him, love Him. We are so buried in ritual that we no longer have a relationship.

Prayer is all relationship.

It is about bringing before our God the fullness of our flesh, the wholeness of our unholy. It is about understanding His intense interest in hearing from each and every one of us, the way He lingers on our every word. It is about knowing the way that He responds to prayer, the way He answers our hearts, the way He comes.

Did you know God still comes?

Most of us don't. Most of us gave up a long time ago on ever experiencing the presence of God like we read in the Bible. We've labored and learned and studied and devoted ourselves to finding Him in prayer the way so many characters in Scripture have done, and He's not here. He hasn't come. He's not coming.

Oh, but He is. He is coming.

The stories in the chapters to follow are here to show you this truth – that God hears you and He's coming. These stories, taken from the pages of the Bible, demonstrate the heart of God to hear His people in prayer and to answer, to come as they call Him.

It is my prayer that as you read these stories, as you engage with the prophets and the priests and the peasants, that you won't focus so much on what they said or how they said it or this or that detail about their prayer.

This is not about polishing the formula. It's not about renovating the ritual.

I want you to pay attention to two simple things – their open hands, the honest, unpretentious ways these men and women came before their God and the incredible, gracious, powerful way that God holds, fills, and honors those hands.

I want you to think about what it would mean to your prayer, to your life, to come with open hands before your God. I want you to consider what it would mean if you sacrificed the ritual for the relationship and came to God not as you think you should come but simply as you are. I want you to think about what it would take for you to unfold your hands and let the God who stands before you take your hands in His.

This is a journey I have been on in my pursuit of powerful prayer. These are the stories and lessons that have spoken to my heart as I have thought about what it must mean to pray. These are the truths that have revolutionized what happens in the space between me and God, where we come together in the fullness of each other's presence and talk in the way I have always wanted to talk to God. When I pray the way my heart tells me to pray. Eyes wide open, face-to-face, holding out my open hand to the God who hears me.

This is prayer the way I always imagined it.

Let us pray...

# \ The Power of Prayer /

There is indescribable power in honest prayer.

It is the power to bring holy fire on the offering of one true prophet standing against hundreds of false ones. It is the power to close a hungry lion's mouth and lay him out like a kitten before a righteous man. It is the power to cast a contrary spirit out of a man and into a pig. It is the power to bear a child from a barren womb.

We are looking for that power. We want to pray the prayer where God shows up. The prayer where He answers us with an undeniable shaking of the earth or tearing of the curtain. Something that will allow us to say that this is our God and He is every bit as real, as authentic, as powerful, and as loving as He promises.

We desperately want to pray those powerful prayers, but we continue to fall tragically short. It seems God rarely hears us or worse, refuses to answer.

Why?

Because we place too much emphasis on getting prayer "right." We study and sermon and agonize over the way we should pray. We have drawn our conclusions and tried to discipline ourselves into praying the "right" way. We pray with our heads bowed. With our hands folded. We fall on our knees for added emphasis. Lift our hands to the Heavens. Pray alone, in a quiet place. In the hustle and bustle of the world. With the television running in the background. With a group of friends. With our families, holding hands around the dinner table.

We focus more on the ritual of prayer than the relationship.

And we have convinced ourselves that just because we call it prayer, it's just that easy. When we ask, we receive. When we seek, we find. When we knock, He opens the door. But the longer we knock without hearing the gears in the lock turn, the more doubt creeps in until we start to wonder if there is power in prayer at all. We wonder if God even hears us.

> What is the difference between honest prayer and right prayer? The simple difference is this: one exists and the other doesn't.

Then, in desperation, when our greatest efforts have failed and we grieve over not seeing the power of prayer in our lives, we either give up and sacrifice prayer on the altar of our flesh or we cry out in pure agony, an unscripted prayer that God would teach us to pray.

It is that prayer that is our most honest, though we fully acknowledge it may have been least "right."

But it is here where we start to hear God answer.

Because the power is not in the practice of prayer; it is in the posture of prayer. It is contained not in the words but in the heart. When we dare to cry out, His power responds. God answers honest prayer, not right prayer.

What is the difference between honest prayer and right prayer? The simple difference is this: one exists and the other doesn't. There is no such thing as right prayer, no magic formula that will curry God's favor. There is no checklist for ensuring we are heard by God.

Honest prayer, however…honest prayer will turn God's ear.

Honest prayer doesn't think about how it's going to play out. It doesn't calculate its words, modify its presentation, and analyze itself to death in the afterthoughts.

Honest prayer is spoken out of a defenseless heart. It is a simple crying out. It is prayer of surrender, an offering to God. To this, He is able to give back the fullest measure. To this, He is able to answer. And He does.

His Word is full of the answer to honest prayer. Honest prayer calms the storm. Honest prayer turns the tide. Honest prayer gives sight to the blind, sound to the deaf, speech to the mute. Honest prayer raises the dead.

Honest prayer is power.

It is this kind of prayer that Jesus was speaking about when He told the disciples, "If you have faith the size of a mustard seed, you can move this mountain." Honest faith, not a contrived faith. Real faith, not just the word.

And when He said, "Seek, ask, knock…and you will find. You will be answered," He was teaching about honest prayer. Seek because you are seeking, ask because you want to know, knock because you want to be let in. It's not enough to just come; come in the fullness of your heart, and the Lord will answer you.

Honest prayer. Real power. It's a promise.

*pray*

Yet it is this power, this promise, that makes us reconsider our honest prayer. On the verge of crying out, we second-guess ourselves. We turn our eyes away, lower our heads, and repent of whatever we were about to ask of our God.

The questions of our heart come washing over us. We question our worthiness to approach His throne. We question our wisdom, that what we would ask is really worth asking. We question God's nature, wondering whether He's still there, still hears us, is tired of our asking, resents our fallenness. We question until there's barely a shred of our honest prayer left to remind us what we were questioning in the first place.

Then we modify our prayer to answer our fear, turning honest prayer into an attempt at right prayer.

If we're going to ask for something so critical, we hesitate. We want to make sure we get it absolutely right.

Our prayer becomes more about the power in us than the power in God.

No wonder we are disappointed.

The incredible power of God and the promise that He will use it should make us rethink our idle prayers, the prayers we pray out of habit instead of holiness. The idle words we mutter. The hollow benedictions we recite. The time we spend going through a list of friends to bless, enemies to curse, situations to heal, and gifts to bestow. The prayers we pray and then immediately forget, questioning in our minds if we have said our prayer today or not. Like trying to remember if we took our medicine, closed the gate, locked the door, put the leftovers back in the refrigerator. Did we pray?

> Our prayer becomes more about the power in us than the power in God.

Knowing the power in prayer absolutely must change our attitude about this mindless prayer. Mindless prayer is useless. Worse, it is fruitless. It does nothing but make us question ourselves, our God, our relationship, our understanding.

But the real power in honest prayer should never make us hesitate. It should not be a barrier between our honest heart and God's. The intimidating power of prayer should not stand between here and the Promise.

Unfortunately, too often, we let it. We let the power of prayer stand in the way because we are afraid. The whisper in our heart that says we are not worthy, not wise, not right to be asking such things. Our heart isn't sure it is ready for this.

What if we did move a mountain?

What if we demanded God show us this mountain and that He move it at our command? Then we woke up the next morning (we always give God until the next morning) and the news announced that the most bizarre thing has happened – a mountain has moved. To the middle of the desert. Inexplicably, it has simply moved.

Wouldn't it be cool, we think, to know we had done that? That's a party story. That's a tale you tell over and over again, and somehow this boosts your own image. Because we would definitely turn it around. We would put it on us, saying that we had prayed for such a thing and neglecting to add that God had answered. We prayed for that mountain to move and bam! There it is. It would be a witness of our own ego instead of our Father's abiding promise.

But it would place a tremendous burden on us, we realize, if we had the power to move a mountain. If we can move a mountain, what other big things can we accomplish through faith? Knowing we could move the mountain would awaken in us the power of the heavens, the strength of the Father living in us. It would tempt us to ego, taunt us to demand more.

And what other big things would God dare ask of us if He knew we firmly believed?

Upon further consideration, we decide we wouldn't really want it to move. The burden would be too great, and to what end? What difference does it make if the mountain is here or there?

It is a sobering moment. It is a moment where we realize the feebleness of our own wisdom. We start to question everything we would pray for, debating back and forth in our hearts whether this would truly be good. Whether this would do as we had hoped it would do. Would it heal or glorify? Would it break and darken? Would it be a burden or a blessing? Or would it bless us? We suddenly don't know any more whether we are asking for something worthy or something less. And we have even less an idea whether it would be in God's will. The mountain may move, but does it matter?

Most never wonder; so few of us have seen a mountain move. But for those who have prayed with the faith of a mustard seed, the power of prayer becomes a haunting insecurity. Do we know what we are asking for?

Just as we start to open our mouths, to ask for something we think would be wonderful, we pause and question what it would mean. What if that situation worked out that way? What if God gave me just what I requested? What if the mountain moved?

*pray*

Jesus said simply to ask, and He would answer. What if we did ask…and He answered? That's too much for our flesh to bear.

Like pupils in a classroom, a few will risk to raise their hand and beg the question.

Where are we going? For what are we purposed? What is it that He is doing in our lives? Will we ever find a spouse, build a family, restore a relationship, heal a wound? What can we do to live more worthy, more holy?

What is it that we are holding onto that is keeping us from surrendering our hearts? What is holding us back from fullness?

A few will ask, but most of us won't because even as our hearts yearn to know the Truth, we are afraid of what He might say. We know He is a true friend, and we know that true friends never lie. They tell you when your hair looks wild, when your clothes hang the wrong way, when you're trailing toilet paper behind your shoe. They tell you when you're being an idiot, when you're standing in your own way, and when you're harming those around you without even knowing it.

They tell you when you're overpowering, when you're too reserved, when you're just plain annoying and need to go away for awhile. They answer your deepest, hardest questions. A good friend tells you the truth, and Jesus is a Good Friend.

> A good friend tells you the truth, and Jesus is a Good Friend.

It is intimidating, but this is why we can be so bold in asking when that gnawing pain in our hearts grows excruciatingly sharp. We can dare ask Him what we're missing, what He sees that we do not, what He's doing that we've been reluctant to follow. We can ask Him to answer the depths of our hearts.

We can ask, knowing He will answer. In raw, painful, penetrating truth. He's not going to go easy on us; He's after our hearts. If we open that up to Him, He's going to demand more from us. He's going to show us where we're shallow, where we're hollow, and where we're lame.

He's also, though, going to show us where we're going, where He will hallow us, and where we will be strong beyond our wildest imagination.

It may sound like criticism. A biting insult that is personally offensive, degrading, and defeating.

Is this supposed to be our Friend?

His answer, though, is love. His answer is promise. His answer is power.

It is not power that comes from the right words, the right posture, or whatever; our Friend answers in the power of prayer that comes from the Lord who hears when we pray.

That is our misunderstanding. We have stepped back, afraid of the power we have in honest prayer. Afraid of the burden it might put on us to have that power.

But our offering of honest prayer does not put the power of the universe in us; it gives what little of our power we count on back to God.

It is a surrender, a confession of faith. It is a humbling of our flesh before His Spirit and an invitation to the power of Truth.

There is power only in prayer that surrenders fully to God. Any other word is powerless.

Every Biblical prayer that demonstrates the power of God proves this is truth. Not one of these prayers depends on a magic formula or a perfect ritual. They are simply words of faith spoken out of defenseless hearts. They are cryings out of the spirit, surrenders of the flesh, pleadings of the heart offered freely to a God.

These prayers teach us to pray purely, to stand before our God in humbled submission and call on His power. Power that will answer when we pray an honest prayer.

# \ Superstition /

When we fail to engage in honest prayer, what would be our petition becomes nothing more than superstition. Nothing more than black cats and broken mirrors and walking under ladders.

We're not folding our hands; we're crossing our fingers. (Although, if we're being honest, we've all prayed a few times with our fingers crossed.)

It offends our sensibilities to think we would ever put prayer in the same category as stepping over cracks in the sidewalk. You just don't put God in the same sentence as the dime in the cabbage. This is faith. This is belief. This is the actual, believable, real God.

He absolutely is.

But our shallow prayer absolutely isn't. Our shallow prayer is superstition at its best, and for evidence of that we need look no further than the definition of superstition.

Webster's defines superstition as *beliefs or practices resulting from ignorance, fear of the unknown, or trust in magic or chance.*[1]

These are the very reasons we revert to shallow prayer - ignorance of what God desires from us, fear of the unknown (or unpredictable) God, and trust in a magic ritual – a "right" way to pray.

*pray*

We are ignorant of what relationship with God means. We don't know what He wants from us, or expects from us. Is the aching of our hearts a prayer He would expect us to pray or does He want more from His children? These petty concerns we so often have – things like money or health or fortune or even family – these pale in comparison to the great majesty that is our Lord. We feel foolish praying about them because they just don't seem like the kind of thing that God would be interested in.

And why should He be? These are not eternal things. These are not holy things. Most of the time, they aren't even necessarily righteous things. It's just that they seem like such big things to us; they seem like our world. We want to pray about them. Our hearts ache over them. But when we finally give in and drop to our knees, we feel like we're ruining prayer by talking about such temporal trash.

The very fact that we spend so much time wondering what God will think of our prayer when He hears it declares our ignorance of the very nature of the God to whom we pray. Or rather, to whom we ought to be praying and kind of sort of hope that we're talking to.

That we worry that our pure heart is not enough for Him shows that we have a lot of misunderstandings about the God who created these very hearts.

That we're concerned that the prayers we long to pray would somehow be displeasing to God displays that we don't know how deeply He loves us.

We don't know Him. We don't know the agony He put into creating us precisely this way. We don't know the painful ache with which He loves us. We forget the blood, sweat, and tears He poured out on the Cross and poured into us.

Blood He poured even into our little things.

We're haunted by the big stories in Scripture, the grand prayers people prayed in tough circumstances, and we convince ourselves that God is only into the big things. Big things we are unlikely to face. Heavy burdens we are unlikely to carry. Hard situations we are unlikely to be in. These are not the things we would pray about on any given day; this is not our life. Our real life, our little things, pale in comparison.

Thankfully, God's Word tells just as many stories of the little things.

For example, Ruth. Ruth is a woman we can relate to. She was a wife and mother who had given up her home for her husband's. Her husband died, and she found herself suddenly alone and unsure which way to go, stuck in a land that was not her own. She wandered back toward something she knew, not knowing for sure what she'd actually do once she got there. She worried about clothes on her back, a roof over her head, and food on her table.

Sound familiar? We are a people who sometimes struggle alone in this world. We are a people constantly worried about where we will go, what we will do, who we will trust. We are concerned about our basic comforts, about our wardrobe and our mortgage and our groceries. These are precisely the things we want to pray about, but the things we feel foolish even mentioning to God.

If God didn't share our concern for such things, why would He share with us the story of Ruth? Her story simply reminds us that God remembers the day-to-day. The kinds of things we're actually likely to face. And He cares.

Or what about the woman at the well, who is engaged in face-to-face conversation with Jesus? She discovers He is the Messiah and her response, still, is to ask for living water, which she thinks is probably like regular water except that she won't have to walk back and forth to this well every day. She's focused on her immediate need, even looking into the eyes of the immeasurable, and He is faithful to answer her.

Or the thief on the cross. He finds himself urgently facing his demise as a consequence of his own hand, his own sinfulness. There's not a lot of time to beat around the bush, but like us, he's not really sure what to say. So he sticks up for Jesus and then turns to the Christ and says, "I know I'm not you. I'm a worse man. And maybe it's too late for this, but there's got to be something better for me. I don't want to damn myself forever here, if there's anything I can do…."

Ever prayed a frantic prayer, overwhelmed by your realization of your brokenness? Yes? That is the prayer of this man, this petty thief, and God's answer to Him is "Today, you will be with me in paradise."

God is all about answering common men and women – Ruth, the nameless woman, the crucified thief, you, me – in common places – a town, a field, a well, a house, death row – with common concerns – food, clothing, shelter, water, comfort, life.

> God is all about answering common men and women – Ruth, the nameless woman, the crucified thief, you, me.

He answers these men and women, not because their prayers were so big or so righteous or so expected but because their hearts were so heavy. The words they dared speak, the trust they put in His hands, was raw and honest. So He came; He answered. And He will answer us if we pray with our hearts.

That is what He wants more than anything. He wants our hearts. He wants our trust. He wants all we've got even when we think it's all just little things. If it's big to us, He says, then it matters to Him. Pray it out.

We trade ignorance for knowledge when we realize we can openly, honestly pray even our little big things.

*pray*

Maybe we're ready to come in honest prayer, big prayer about a little thing that's so big to us, but superstition stops us again. We don't know how God will answer, and that's a scary proposition. If we can bring our hearts to push aside ignorance and embrace the reality of relationship with God as His highest priority, we have lingering questions about what that looks like.

Who is this God who is listening? Who is this God who answers?

We want a God of grace who will simply forgive us and restore us to His favor. The God who looked at a woman bowed at His feet, perfume in her hair, who had not spoken a word of prayer, and told her, "Your sins are forgiven." That's the God we want.

We want the God who heard the blind man beg for sight, gave him sight, and didn't give him grief about it.

The God we fear will answer us, however, is the God of David and Job who was, shall we say, a bit more harsh.

David, a man of devout prayer, sinned against the Lord by taking a census. He then returned to the Lord and prayed his repentance, that God would forgive him for his sinful deed.

In response, God gave David three choices: seven years of famine, three months of pursuit by enemies, or three days of plague. (2 Samuel 24:10-14)

This doesn't exactly make us want to come honestly before God with a confession of our sins. This doesn't make us want to open our hearts and be honest with Him. With trouble in our hearts, we're afraid that if we come to Him, this is the God we are going to find. A God of undesirable consequences. Famine, persecution, or plague? Really? What happened to grace?

Job cried out in raw, honest prayer about the very things we want to pray about – family, friends, possessions, life in general, suffering, misery, pain. He had questions. The God who answered Him did not pat Job on the shoulder and say, "There, there." He argued with the troubled man.

> We'd rather pray shallow than open our lives to the havoc of a God we can't predict.

"Who is this that belittles my advice with words that do not show any knowledge about it? Brace yourself like a man! I will ask you, and you will teach me," God says to Job before proceeding to ask him endless questions about creation, creating, righteousness, justice, the heavens, the earth, and everything else. (Job 38)

If we're going to bring our hearts to God, we want to know He won't just argue with us.

Fearing what God might do when we give Him our hearts, it's hard to stay on our knees in honest prayer. We'd rather pray shallow than open our lives to the havoc of a God we can't predict. We hem and haw and beat around the bush because we're not sure what would happen if we simply said it.

That's no way to pray.

We have to stop focusing on the God we cannot predict and dive into His word to discover the deeper truth about who He is. In the overall, broadest, most eternal and timeless exposition of our God, who is He?

He is the God who answered Job with questions. But also the God who answered Hannah with a son. He is the God who answered David with a plague. But also the God who anointed him. He is the God who answered Israel with the wilderness. But also the God who showed them the Promised Land.

When we uncover the full picture of God and His interaction with His people, we find no reason to be afraid. He is no longer unknown, but known. Not only known, but trusted. Not only trusted, but loved. By love, we are able to give Him our honest prayer and not worry about what He will do with our hearts.

He will love them, we know. Tenderly. Mercifully. Fully.

We trade fear for faith when we understand the true nature of the God who answers.

*pray*

The third component of superstition, and perhaps the most dangerous, is our trust in magic or chance. This is the epitome of the ritualized prayer. This is the reason we're so concerned about getting our prayer "right."

We've convinced ourselves that God has a magic word. A prestidigious posture. A certain expectation of our prayer that, if we put the pieces together in just the right way, we will curry His favor and earn His answer.

It's merely chance that we would ever stumble upon this magic formula, but that doesn't keep us from trying. We take every prayer from Scripture, diagram and dissect it to discover its "magic," confabulate all of our inferences together into a single picture of what a "right" prayer must be, and set about to meet those criteria, if we can even remember them all when we finally fall to our knees.

We want to pray with the boldness of David, the repentance of Jonah, the faith of Abraham, the wisdom of Solomon, the confidence of Daniel, the graciousness of Paul, the surrender of Jesus, and the many other characteristics of God's characters in prayer that we so admire throughout Scripture. We want to pray like the men and women of God who heard His answer.

In trying to pray like them, we more often end up simply stealing their prayers. This becomes our ritual. Their prayers seem so much greater than anything we could put together ourselves. And they heard God answer, so obviously their prayers were right. The magic of prayer must be somewhere in those words.

The so-called magic of these prayers is not in the words; it is in the hearts that spoke them. These men and women, without exception, were praying out of their own hearts with their own words and without caring what anyone else may or may not have prayed once upon a time. They made no room for ritual or rote.

They knew the Scriptures; they could have stalked a winning prayer the same way we do. Joel could have asked for the answers of Elijah. Samuel could have asked for the answers of Moses. Joseph could have asked for the answers of Abraham. None of them did.

Each man, each woman prayed in their own words from their own heart because they wanted to hear from *their* God. They wanted the God who made them, loved them, and heard them to answer them.

If we want the God who made us, loves us, and hears us to answer, then we have to pray our own words. From our own hearts.

## Superstition

We want every bit of God to meet every bit of us, and when we confine ourselves to a ritualized prayer, we inevitably push aside a piece of our heart that is longing for Him.

We pray the Lord's Prayer. We pray to hallow His name. We pray for forgiveness and daily bread. But what are we supposed to do with a heart that doesn't fit in these categories? What do we do with that very real ache that just can't settle for bread?

It's the Lord's Prayer! we argue. Forgiveness, daily bread…this is all we need.

Maybe. But it is not all we want. We want more.

We want God. We want the God who created us to make sense of our creation. We want the God who knows us to anticipate what we need. We want the God who loves us to stand beside us. We want the God who died for us to walk where we live. We want the God who hears us to answer us, whether on any given day we're satisfied with bread or hungry for something more.

> But what are we supposed to do with a heart that doesn't fit in these categories? What do we do with that very real ache that just can't settle for bread?

We do not meet that God in ritual or rote; we can only find Him in relationship. When we stop trusting in magic words and dare to compose a new prayer. From our own hearts. In our own times. In our own circumstances. In our own words.

In a prayer of petition.
Beyond superstition.

## \ Honest Prayer /

Honest prayer is not as difficult as we make it. It first flows freely, but we are so trapped in our teachings that we convince ourselves to make honest prayer more "right." We turn it into a template, a prayer that can be clearly defined and replicated - words to remember, postures to assume, scripts to follow until our once honest prayer becomes our trusted rote prayer. Then we pray those "better" words over and over again, waiting on nothing to happen.

Because until we set our hearts free of the ritual and cry out thirsty, that is what will happen – nothing.

God just doesn't care for our rituals. He doesn't care for our formulas. He doesn't care for our formalizations. Of all of the powerful prayers in Scripture that we so admire, not one begins with a folding of the hands, a bowing of the head, a closing of the eyes, and a deferent, "Dear Lord, we come before you now humbly and in awe of your tender mercies…."

No! The prayers of the Bible start with an agonized "Lord!" with all the heartache of a child standing alone. Then pour out a raw and honest heart.

That is honest prayer. And we are falling short.

We aren't letting ourselves cry out.

Because most of us are questioning. We're trying to figure out how in a world of impurities, we have a God so pure. We're trying to discover how in a world of insecurities, we have a God so consistent. We're trying to fathom how, as intimately as we know our imperfect hearts, He would love us anyway with a perfect love.

We're questioning how in a world to the contrary, God could be as He says He is. He proclaims an almost unfathomable goodness. Dare we believe?

It is a tough question. If we cry out with all that we are, and God does not answer.... Unanswered prayer could shatter our faith.

Yet we long to believe. It is why we keep praying, why we keep asking God to show Himself as hope He would be. Prayer is our invitation to God to show up and show us what our hearts are holding onto – that there is Truth. That there is something real beyond all this mess. That there is a good and gracious God who hears and who answers His children. That He is our personal good and gracious God.

It's easy to look at the way things are, this world we live in, and say that the one standing alone is an anomaly. It's much harder to look at the One standing alone and think He might be onto something.

But He has to be! We ache for Him to be. We keep praying so that we give Him every chance, every invitation to be. To really be the One that stands against. To really be the One we believe in. To be the God of the Bible here in the flesh.

In our flesh, Lord, if You please. Be God in our flesh.

*pray*

We ache in honest prayer, but still we question. We question whether God will even hear us, whether He will answer. It is the blurring of insecurities; from an insecure world, we breed an insecure faith.

It is a faith that has asked, but not received. It is a faith that has knocked and stood at the door like a fool. It is a faith that has sought, but never found. It is a faith that has poured out its heart and heard nothing but silence.

Yet it is a faith that refuses to die.

We get angry. We question. We want to question our God.

Instead, we question ourselves.

We question what we have prayed, concluding it was more whim than wisdom. We question the way we prayed, knowing how easily distracted we are. We question the words of our prayer, wishing they were more holy. We agonize over our scripted prayers and our practiced posture.

In times when faith stands waiting, our powerless prayer lets us say that we are the problem. Our ritual lets us say that we fell short. The science of the perfect prayer lets us comb back over every tiny detail of our posture and our words and find the place where we messed up, where we were less than worthy, where we strayed.

God is still God, but we messed up and failed to connect with Him. Our unworthiness, our inability, our shortcoming hindered God in hearing us; we could not have expected Him to answer.

As defeating as these questions are, it is much easier, and much less devastating, to question ourselves than to question our God.

> It is a faith that has asked, but not received. It is a faith that has knocked and stood at the door like a fool. It is a faith that has sought, but never found.

If it is we who fail, we get to hold onto this image of God that fuels our hearts and infuses our monotony with meaning. We get to believe that He is who He says He is, as long as we can figure out how to be who we ought to be.

As long as we can figure out how to pray right.

*pray*

Right prayer is a frustrating venture. We try, but we continue to fail. We try to prove our worth, but we find no worthiness in us. The standards are too high, we fume. God is never going to hear us. He will never answer. This is an impossible task.

Who among us can pray a right prayer?

But we're never ready to give up. We're reluctantly relenting and ready to try it again, to show Him we will keep working to get it right while we pull out our notes and put our prayer under a magnifying glass. We're thirsty for God to be God, and we're determined to make our prayers worthy to deserve Him. We pray failed prayer after failed prayer, playing with our hearts and our words, and decide that if we try long enough, He will answer. His mercy will overcome Him and He will respond, even though we still fall short of praying right.

While we study and scrutinize and struggle to pray again, increasingly believing it is all in vain, it is not God's mercy but His heartache that overcomes Him. He cries out to us, "What is it you want? Look up, and just tell Me already!"

We hear His agonized plea, longing to hear from us, begging us to just talk with Him, and we get flustered. In a moment of promise, having heard His voice, knowing He is listening, anxious for the opportunity to speak…we clasp our hands, lower our heads, and begin, "Oh, uh, Lord. I mean, Dear Heavenly Father…."

And God says, "Don't take that tone with Me."

The Eternal is calling out to us, and we're still more concerned with our process than our purity. Our hearts are aching, thirsty for a touch from the Father, longing for Eden, burdened beyond understanding, and here He stands waiting while we burden ourselves to get it right!

This emphasis we put on getting it right, on proving ourselves worthy even to ask, has turned our prayers into habit instead of honor, ritual instead of relationship. We tiptoe around, trying to demonstrate respect and deference, instead of crying out when God is begging us to just spill our hearts already.

The Heavens groan. Our hearts ache.

God hates to tell us this (lest we put an even bigger burden on ourselves to get it right), but it *is* us. This is *our* shortcoming. But it's not our form or our formula; it is our force. **We're trying too hard.**

> God hates to tell us this...but it *is* us. We're trying too hard.

When you strain to lift a weight that is more than your muscles can handle, your eyes kind of go crossed and everything gets a little fuzzy right before pass out. It's the same with our prayer – we're trying to lift a burden that is beyond our strength, and our eyes are getting all fuzzy. "Right" prayer is a heavy burden. It blurs our eyes until we cannot see the God standing in front of us, the God who is answering our heart.

He's easy to miss, particularly when we are trapped in the ritual of right prayer. Because the answer to right prayer, we suppose, is a right response – one very specific, pre-defined outcome that we have determined is the only possible confirmation that God had heard us, that He will answer us, and even that He is good. By our wisdom, we know what the answer is. Getting that answer, that precise answer, becomes blindingly important and we can't even remember why we wanted it except that now, we want it because we want God to answer us. And getting the right answer means we have prayed right.

God is going to answer, but He's not going to leave us hungry. He's not going to give us the answer that has blinded us to the question; He's going back to the heart of our prayer, the honesty of it that fell by the wayside in our exasperated efforts to get it right and to define in concrete, unchangeable terms exactly what is an "answer." *The* answer, because we will accept only one.

That one may or may not be coming. In God's wisdom, it may or may not be the answer. It may or may not actually be right. But God will do right by us if we open our eyes to see what He is doing. When we let His answer, which often seems so wrong, sink into our hearts, we find His promise all over again. We find His goodness. We find His heart, wrapped in an answer.

It is right.

And we never had to work for it.

*pray*

Honest prayer is not about setting aside a certain time and place, bowing our heads and folding our hands and blocking out the distractions of a world moving on around our stillness.

It's not about copying some template from the Bible. There's no pattern to prayer that makes God answer. There's no instruction on writing a form letter to God.

There are only two words the Bible gives us to call on the name of God:

Cry out.

Cry out. That's what we love about prayers like the Psalms - they are raw. They are real. That's what God loves about them, too.

He loves it when we do the same.

Honest prayer is about purity. Not that we would be pure, but that we would come pure. It is about praying our thirst, our hunger, our desperate longings. It is about praying out of an open heart. It is about connecting the space between here and There, the time between now and Then, the mortality of this and the eternity of That.

Honest prayer has questions. We always have questions. But honest prayer brings our questions to God instead of using them to build a barrier between us. Honest prayer will ask, trusting that God will answer. Even if it's not the answer the heart was hoping for.

Honest prayer will seek, trusting that God will reveal.

Honest prayer will knock, trusting God will let us in.

Honest prayer cries out, knowing God is listening. Knowing He hears. Knowing that *something* will happen.

Because in response to honest prayer, something always has.

## \ Demand Fullness /

What happens in response to honest prayer is not necessarily what happens *next*. It is one of the greatest lies about prayer in our generation, this "must be God's will" principle that convinces us to settle for a God whose answer is a firm no, a deafening silence, or a lesser blessing.

We have been taught to believe – and have bought the lie – that God might be answering our prayer, just in unexpected ways. Desperate to be heard, longing to be answered, we start looking for things we would never believe are God's holy will. Our hearts jump at any sign of the unexpected. We are willing to believe that whatever happens immediately after we pray, whatever develops in the situation or the heart or the terror that we have prayed over, is His will. It is His answer.

Even when it doesn't seem like an answer at all.

We settle for less. Less than we had prayed for. Less than we had hoped from a God who claimed to love us. We take it because we believe it is all He is giving, but we cannot shake the disappointment that He isn't giving more.

We thought our prayer was earnest. We thought our hearts were right. We risked approaching the Throne of Heaven to expose our vulnerabilities, to seek mercy and grace. Then whatever we have ended up with must be that mercy. It must be that grace. And if we embrace it – as backward, as far-fetched, as half-hearted as it may seem – then in time, we will see the wisdom even in this.

That is what we tell ourselves, and our thirsty souls drink that up for the chance to say we have been visited by our God. A God we suspected all along was personal. A God we expected all along cared about us. A God we prayed to, believing He would answer.

But it is a God we have sacrificed on the altar of impatience. A God we have given up for one taste of anything, something that will satisfy our ever-seeking hearts.

> We explain our disappointment away with theological platitudes and long-sermoned truths.

This is not a Biblical perspective. It is the sight given us by our culture, our hurried pace that would rather take what is now than wait for something better and our false sense of meekness that dares not speak up and demand anything more.

While we will loudly defend ourselves and tout our worthiness for social gain, in employment, with our families or even to stave off the unworthy feeling deep in our hearts, we have been taught with God to be thankful for what we are given, to quiver before Him, so we take with a grumbled thanks whatever comes our way and adjust our faith accordingly.

We explain our disappointment away with theological platitudes and long-sermoned truths – that God knows better than we know and our prayer was ill-conceived, at best. That God, by answering in just this way, has set our hearts toward higher things, even though they seem much lower. That God seeks to bestow on us wisdom instead of whimsy and that we will thank Him for this one day.

Just not today.

*pray*

Look back over the thousands of powerful prayers spoken in His Word. There is not one man, woman, or child passionately pursuing God's heart who stops when the first "answer" comes along, throws out their deepest heart, shrugs a shoulder, and says, "Well, thanks God. I suppose I'll see the wisdom in this some day."

No! They press on, and the weak imposter of answered prayer only implores them to greater earnestness, to deeper yearning, and to a more powerful encounter with God.

Mark tells the story of a blind man brought to Jesus by his well-intentioned friends. (8:22-26) The setting is Bethsaida, and just as Jesus arrives, so does this posse, ushering the blind man closer and closer to the famed Teacher. They have heard of His healing touch. Word arrived long before He did, and they were waiting.

We don't know what the man's thoughts were. Was he afraid to go with his friends? Did he know where they were leading him? Not once does Mark say that this man was eager or anxious or doubtful or anything. Not once are we told he speaks a word on his own behalf. The man is silent.

If he was anything like us, he probably had his hesitations. Maybe he had spent too many nights praying to a God he now thought would never answer him. A God who perhaps he thought could not answer him. Maybe he knew his own heart and feared this Lord would not take the time for him or worse, would scorn him in public and expose his hidden story. Maybe he didn't feel worthy. Maybe he lacked faith. Mark doesn't tell us.

Nevertheless, his friends push him toward the Teacher. Jesus, with great compassion, takes the man by the hand and leads him away. The two walked to a place more private, more quiet, where the crowds were not pressing in, where the friends could not plead the blind man's case. Jesus wanted this man to know that it was just the two of them – broken and Healer. They were removed. They were away. They were alone.

Here, Jesus commits one of His more disgusting acts: He spits on His hands and wipes them on the man's eyes. A healing touch masked in unnecessary slime. Could He not have healed the man with a simple word?

But this is the Rabbi's heart. He wanted the man to know that He was there. He knew the man could not see Him working, and He provided a tangible reassurance that He was still there, that He was willing, and that He would heal. To that man, the touch meant one beautiful thing – the very real presence of a personal Lord whose only heart in that moment was for him.

"Can you see anything now?" Jesus asks the man.

The man probably hesitated. This was the Lord standing before him; he could almost see that now. Yet he knew this healing was not complete. Perhaps he blinked a few times, shook his head around trying to wash the healing over every last bit of his eyes. Perhaps he thought it would take some time, that he should try it out for a few days and see. (Or not see.) Perhaps he wondered what to say, how to respond.

It is a moment we can say, living as we live, that we would have walked away from. We would have taken a half-sighted life over total darkness. We would not dare think in the Lord's presence that His touch had not been good enough. That very thought would force us to question our worthiness, question our intent or desire, question our Lord, and curse ourselves for not being grateful. Who are we to demand more from the Lord?

That moment, though, was the blind man's. It was his with the Lord, and who knew when Jesus would travel back through Bethsaida? Who knew if He would ever return? The chance was now; the time was now. The tenderness in Christ's voice, a Healer who already knew the answer, invited the man to answer in truth.

"Yes," he said. "I see people, but I can't see them very clearly. They look like trees walking around."

Jesus again places His hands on the man's eyes. With that second touch, the man's sight is completely restored. He saw clearly, and for the first time, He saw the face of his Lord.

Now, are we to believe that Jesus could not have healed this man in one touch? Of course not! We know that the power of Jesus is the power of God, the Father in the Son and the Son in the Father, and it would have taken only a word – spoken aloud or spoken in the heart – for this man's sight to be fully restored. There's something more that Jesus wanted to show him here, another lesson from the Teacher.

> This was an opportunity for more than blind faith; He was inviting this man to truly see.

This was an opportunity for more than blind faith; He was inviting this man to truly see.

He wanted this man to engage with Him. He wanted this man to be as fully present, open, and responsive as He was. He wanted this man to dare in faith to hunger for his Lord.

Jesus wasn't just giving it His best shot and walking away, throwing some half-hearted answer at a man locked in darkness, and returning to the throngs of adoring devotees clamoring for His return. He was there, without a thought to anything else, and for that moment intent on giving this man the deepest of everything, the wholeness of presence, and the fullness of healing.

He was inviting this man to acknowledge how the taste of half-sightedness left him thirsting for more.

*pray*

What if the blind man had settled for that first touch? What if he had simply thanked the Lord standing before him for trying? What if he had stopped with his "yes," which was an honest answer to Jesus' question – "Can you see *anything* now?" He easily could have thought, as many of us would, that this was the best his healing would get. This was the power of the touch of Christ in his life. This was the best the presence would get him. This was what God had intended all along.

He would have walked away thirsty, the pang of emptiness intensified by half-fullness. He would have stumbled back to his friends with a story of a touch and the evidence of a less-than God.

And he would have walked away never seeing the Lord not two feet in front of him, fully present, fully engaged with one man while the world stood off at a distance, no doubt still pressing in, trying to get to this Teacher, trying to see what was going on.

What a tragedy!

That Man, two feet in front of him, feet dirty and hands damp is the real gift here. Not the gift of sight, though we know how that changed this blind man's life. His sight restored, he could return to his family, to his work, to his community and be an active participant in life. His friends no longer had to carry his burden; they didn't have to lead him around or feel guilty about leaving him to sit, lost, in the city. Certainly, the renewal of his eyes was a tremendous, life-changing gift.

But the presence of God was greater still. The comfort of knowing the Lord was there. The stillness of being alone with Him. The way the Lord made a point of walking this man away from the noise, from the crowds, from the busyness of everything and carving out the time and place for just the two of them. The tenderness of His touch, the gentleness of His voice.

This man walked away seeing. But he also walked away knowing that Jesus healed him not for the fame, not for the pleasure of the crowds, not to silence his friends or the Pharisees or His persecutors. He had healed him just for him. This man walked away with the deepest knowledge of Presence. Individual, personal presence.

We would have walked away with much less. We would have settled. We are settling.

When it comes to our prayer, to our greatest needs, to our deepest desires, we are all too quick to settle for whatever comes first. Whatever happens after we pray, we convince ourselves is God's full will for us. It is His answer. It is the best we will get out of Him, and it is non-negotiable.

These small tokens, these half-answers, we treasure as something tangible of our God. Were the blind man to have taken his half-sight and walked away, he no doubt would have looked at every walking tree with the memory of a moment with God. He would have stumbled through a hazy world with eyes covered in holy spit, savoring a presence that he felt but never saw. But he would have never seen what the God who stood before him really looked like.

That is our trouble. We walk away with half-answered prayer and take with us a blurred image of God.

We walk away not knowing what He looks like.

When we take an answer that seems less than good, we question what goodness looks like. When we take an answer less than whole, we question what power looks like. When we expect God to fashion an answer just for us and something generic falls into our laps, we question the creativity of our Creator. When we take the natural consequence as more than the law of nature, we question the very nature of the supernatural. Suddenly, God doesn't seem so God-like.

> Suddenly, God doesn't seem so God-like.

What, then, are we to say of our God when we have walked away not knowing Him? When we have walked away with a lesser picture of our Creator, what are we to say to those watching? What are we to say to a world longing to see the Lord, waiting for us to come back and show them something of the Magnificent?

Had the man walked back to his friends half-sighted and faced their questions about this famed Jesus, how could he have answered?

"Uhm, He's...wet."

Wet, because the man only knew a slimy, half-healing touch. Because he could only see a shadowy figure standing before him that he might easily mistake for a tree. Because he'd missed out on the fullness of the Lord's presence and wouldn't dare tell the crowds this Jesus could not heal him. They had seen the Teacher work miracles; if His power was insufficient, it must be the man's fault, not the Lord's. All this man would have had short of words inciting a riot was "wet."

There would have been no follow-up, no press conference, no Q & A about the private moment. The man would have slinked away through the crowds, shaking his head and wondering what these people saw in this Rabbi.

But this man had more than "wet." He had an encounter. He had a moment where he chose to speak truth, where he wasn't intimidated by rumors of God's goodness or his own known inadequacy as a man. A moment where he chose to say, "It is good, Lord, but I am thirsty for more." A moment where God honored his tenacity and *healed him*.

In that moment, the man gained more than sight.

In that moment, the man gained intimate knowledge of a Lord who heard him. A God committed to fullness in him. A Rabbi whose lesson plan includes a back-and-forth and not a lecture.

What about our moment? Are we walking away knowing the Lord who has heard us? Are we taking with us the image of a God who is committed to us? Do we know that He is inviting us to a conversation as much as a conversion? Do we have more than "wet"?

The sad truth is that many of us are stuck with a one-dimensional, obscure explanation of our God. We are stuck in a place where we struggle to tell others about Jesus because we have to admit we don't understand Him. We struggle to talk about His goodness because we no longer believe He has our best interest at heart. We struggle to talk about His presence because we have settled for less. We struggle to talk about His power because everything sort of looks like trees walking around. We have walked away wet and nothing more.

If we want to encounter the God of the Bible, the God who takes the time to stand alone just He and us, the God who answers the prayer of His children and gives them the greatest, most unfathomable blessings –

sight in the place of blindness, speech in the place of muteness, life in the place of death – we have to be willing to engage Him.

We have to be willing to take His hand, to walk away from the crowds and the noise and the pressure. We have to be willing to pour out our hearts, to speak for ourselves and surrender our broken places to Him. We have to be willing to let Him touch us.

And when we're standing there feeling like the God of the Universe just spit on us, we have to be willing to say, "It is good, Lord, but I am thirsty for more."

# \ Straight Up Pray /

Our hearts ache for more, but we hesitate to tell God we're still thirsty. Instead, we tell ourselves that we must pray "better" prayers.

Like Solomon's prayer for wisdom in 1 Kings 3. God granted him the wisdom that he asked for, then the riches and security that he didn't because, as God said, he honored the Lord by praying not for himself but for something Kingdom-worthy. The result of this righteous prayer was more.

That could be us, we think. We could pray a more holy prayer, one more righteous, and then God could reward us with that good thing and more. We could pray for something noble, then whatever lies beneath our masked prayer (the true desire of our heart, the riches and security we really long for) will come as part of the package.

So we pray for wisdom. Because we're looking for the God of blessings, promise, and reward. We're looking for the God that gives us beyond what we ask for. We're looking for the God our post-modern, self-centered, 21st-Century sense of entitlement tells us is waiting to cater to our whim. And if He's looking for someone who prays for wisdom, then that sounds fairly good to us.

We pray for wisdom. And keep our fingers crossed for so much less.

Or we see David's many psalms, articulate beyond our words, and think that should be us. That we need to find articulate words to pray to God. That a better prayer is a more beautiful-sounding one.

David never backed away from telling God like it was. It sucks down here, Lord, we can imagine him saying, though we would hardly believe such an articulate man would use such an ugly word as "sucks." But I think he would have. It sucks here, God. And just where are You, he would continue. Everybody's after me and I feel so alone and my life doesn't deserve to be this way (except, of course, in the cases where he is admitting that his life absolutely deserves to be that way) and I'm looking for You, God, and where in the heavens are You?

> If we told God like it is and spewed out our lives unedited at the feet of our Father, these wouldn't be words that anyone would emulate; they'd be words we'd be cleaning up. With a mop.

Could you imagine pouring your heart out to God like that? Most of us know that if we tried, if we told God like it is and spewed out our lives unedited at the feet of our Father, these wouldn't be words that anyone would emulate; they'd be words we'd be cleaning up. With a mop.

But David gets away with it, and what's more – he enjoys the richest blessings of God. It has to be in his language, we think. It has to be because his words are beautiful, because he's posed prayer in this incredible poetry that we could only dream of creating.

It is inspiring to watch this man lay down his life – his good and his bad, his ugly and his broken, his frustrations and his spites – at the feet of his God, who David firmly believes is hearing and answering.

It is inspiring to watch God answer him. Abundantly. God granted this wordsmith more.

So we pray with the biggest, grandest, most articulate words we can muster. And realize even we don't know what we're praying.

*pray*

The more the examples of David and Solomon tear at our hearts, the more we find ourselves lost in a muddled prayer somewhere between trying to trick God and trying to impress Him. But these prayers – the prayers of David and Solomon and of many others like them – did neither. They were something much more bold and much less muddled.

They were honest prayers.

Solomon wasn't trying to trick God. He wasn't trying to sound holy, hiding his true desire behind a righteous-sounding curtain. He wasn't harboring a hope for the riches and honor he hadn't asked for. He honestly wanted wisdom.

David wasn't trying to impress God. He wasn't laboring over his word choice, writing and re-writing his prose with a prayer in one hand and a dictionary in the other. His are the raw words of a seeker's heart crying out in unedited, unencumbered honesty.

It's easy to be intimidated by these kings of Israel, these fathers of the faith. Of course two of the most honored men in God's story prayed powerful prayers. But remember that before they were big names, they were little guys. David was a shepherd boy; Solomon wasn't even the rightful heir. These are the men who prayed. They were nobodies; they were anybodies.

Nobodies and anybodies are the men and women we meet in the story of Jesus. Have you noticed how few of them are mentioned by name? Yet each one of them had a powerful encounter with the Son of God, the ambassador of the Father, the flesh of Love come down to answer them. And every encounter began with a nobody asking for his heart without pretense, without tricks, and without any particularly articulate words.

A leper bowed at the feet of Jesus and said, "If you're willing, you can make me clean." (Matthew 8:2b, Mark 1:40b, Luke 5:12) A Roman officer asked Him, "Just give a command, and my servant will be healed." (Matthew 8:8b, Luke 7:7) Two blind men called out, "Have mercy on us, Son of David!" (Matthew 9:27b)

These are neither impressive nor memorable men. They are simply a leper. A Roman officer. Blind men.

A leader in the synagogue pled with Jesus, "Come, lay your hand on [my daughter] and she will live." (Matthew 9:18b, Luke 8:41) Mark adds the small detail that this man's name was Jairus (5:23). Does it matter? Not to most of us.

Maybe to the early readers of Mark's writing, it made a difference. Maybe Jairus was well-known, a great figure in regional history. Maybe everyone knew something about Jairus that would have left them either shocked or encouraged that this man in particular would seek out Jesus.

Or maybe this name – Jairus – helps those early readers connect this story to the headlines. Maybe they'd heard about some miraculous healing of Jairus' little girl, and Mark is simply using this detail to confirm that this is that story.

But today? It doesn't matter whether this man's name was Jairus or Jehoshephat or Fred. We'd consider him a nobody; he could have been anybody.

A Canaanite woman pushed through the crowds, and she really was a nobody. In those days, good Jewish men and women did not associate with such garbage as the Canaanites and even this woman knew that. But she threw herself at Jesus' feet anyway and begged, "Have mercy on me, Lord, Son of David!" And then again, "Lord, help me!" (Matthew 15:22, 25; Mark 7:26, 28) And a third time, after Jesus makes a comment about dogs – referring to the reputation of the Canaanite people - she owns her ethnicity and begs again, "But even the dogs eat scraps that fall from their masters' tables." (Matthew 15:27) Finally, her prayer is answered and her daughter is healed. Answered prayer for an absolute nobody by every definition of the word.

> Jesus preferred nobodies. That's why He picked twelve of them to be His disciples.

*pray*

Jesus preferred nobodies. That's why He picked twelve of them to be His disciples. They seem like a lot more to us because we know them by name, but they wouldn't have impressed anybody in 31 A.D. Galilee. They were just men. Simon and Andrew, James and John were fishermen. Blue-collar workers. Matthew was a tax collector. White-collar guy. Later, Paul was a tentmaker. A craftsman. Maybe today they seem like much more. But they're not.

They're just guys, regular run-of-the-mill anybodies, who just so happened to journey with Jesus.

And when you look at the ways they interacted with Him, they were just as inarticulate and unpretentious as the men and women on the side of the road.

Simon Peter is trapped in a boat being rocked by a storm when he spots Jesus on the horizon and says, "Tell me to come to you on the water." (Matthew 14:28, NIV) Jesus walks into Simon and Andrew's house and we aren't even privy to their words. We are only told that Simon's mother-in-law is sick and that they told Him about her – Mark says, "first thing." (1:30; Luke 4:38) Do you think when they told Him about her illness, they took the time to form what we'd call a proper prayer? Would they have said something like, "O precious, gracious Jesus. We are so honored to have You in our home, and we are thankful for the gift of Your presence here. But we have heavy hearts right now, as our mother lies upstairs with a fever. And we know, Teacher, that You can heal her, as You have healed so many others, and so we ask right now for Your mercy…"

Not a chance. That's not a prayer we see anywhere in the Scriptures, and it's certainly not the one we never get the words for. Their prayer would have been just as the others we've seen – from the blind man, the deaf man, the Canaanite woman, the father, the friends, the nobodies, the anybodies. It would have been, "Jesus, have mercy on our mother!"

And that would have been enough.

That is the prayer that Jesus answered, even if it doesn't seem holy enough for our standards. In all of the Bible, even in the days of this Jesus, God honors the prayers that aren't necessarily articulate and certainly aren't deceptive but are simply honest words from a raw heart that senses it's got one moment, this moment, to have Jesus and isn't about to miss that chance for something so pretentious as trying to sound right.

A blind man on the side of the road has one chance to talk to the passing Jesus. When Jesus asks him what it is that he wants, the man doesn't beat around the bush. "Lord, I want to see again." (Luke 18:41b)

A woman at a well is weary and here she is alone with the famed Teacher for only the few minutes it takes for His disciples to find food. She doesn't have time for details; when He tells her about this thing called living water, she decides. "Give me this water!" (John 4:15)

Near a pool known for its healing waters, a sick man is honest with this Rabbi and speaks from his doubting heart. He doesn't realize the power in the hand that's reaching out to him, but he speaks from his own resignation that healing is just out of touch for him. "I don't have anyone to put me into the pool." (John 5:7) Jesus answers by showing him that he never needed a pool.

Honest, simple words from honest, simple hearts of nobodies who were fully aware of their place in the social structure. They walked away healed. They walked away satisfied. And they walked away knowing there was a God who heard them.

*pray*

Honest, simple words and answered prayer. Men and women receiving from God just what they asked. Yet when we talk about a God who answers prayers, we don't talk about this God. We don't talk about the Healer who faithfully answered the inarticulate prayers of the common man. We talk about the God in 1 Kings 3 who answers prayers and then some, the One who gives Solomon the wisdom that he asks for and the riches that he doesn't. And we're not satisfied with a God who just fulfills.

Honest, simple words and answered prayer. Yet not a prayer in the bunch we try to emulate. Having read the Psalms, we'd never settle for such unadorned words.

These men and women received a full measure of mercy, but that's not enough. We'd rather be impressive. We'd rather our words go down as the words of a person after God's own heart.

Don't you think the crowds were a people after God's own heart? Don't you think the way they flooded the streets, criss-crossed the lake, and traveled for days just to get a glimpse of this Man and pour out their hearts to Him demonstrates at the very least that?

> Jesus isn't impressed. He doesn't care if you're somebody.

But most of us don't want to be a people, even a people after God's own heart; we want to be the man, the woman who He loves. Not one of many, but merely one. Not nobody, not anybody, but somebody.

Jesus isn't impressed. He doesn't care if you're somebody.

A rich young man came to Jesus and asked, "What good deed should I do to gain eternal life?" (Matthew 19:16) This man was a nobody, but he felt like a somebody. When Jesus responded with the law of love and a rehashing of the Ten Commandments, the man asserted, "I do all of this. I always have." He was trying to impress both the crowds and the Teacher. But Jesus wouldn't have it.

"Sell what you own. Give the money to the poor, and you will have treasure in heaven." (v. 21) And the man was crushed. He'd thought God would be impressed with his being somebody, and here was the Son of God telling him to give it all up and be nobody.

Martha, too, thought she was somebody. She had the inside connection with Jesus. So when her brother Lazarus lay dying, she assumed that because she was

Martha, Jesus was going to show up and take care of this as soon as He heard the news. After all, she and Jesus went way back. He would certainly come for a friend and she would get that extra-special touch of bonus God, the God who drops everything and comes racing to her because He loves her so extra-special much.

Then Jesus shows up two days late and Lazarus is lying in a tomb rotting in his flesh, and Martha has the gall to storm out and say, "If you had been here…" (John 11:21) If you had come, Teacher, then Lazarus would still be here. I guess I'm not all that important to you if you can just dilly-dally and take your grand old time when my brother lays dying. And now he's dead.

The same gall, the same tell-it-like-it-is attitude of a David from a somebody who just realized she's an anybody.

An anybody who witnessed one of Jesus' greatest miracles in the resurrection of a man from the dead, but still just an anybody because His answer had nothing to do with her indignation or sense of entitlement. It was just His love.

The same love that answers each anybody and nobody and everybody who cries out to Him, men, women, and children who do not walk away disappointed.

*pray*

Do you think the blind man was disappointed when all that Jesus gave him was sight? Do you think the father wanted anything more than his son back? And the Canaanite woman – did she go home to her child and spend the night lying awake rethinking her words, wishing she had one more chance to say it better?

Of course not. These men and women on the side of the road, pushing through the crowds, laboring to get to Jesus took their raw, honest hearts to the Savior in one holy moment as He passed by in the flesh. And He heard them. And He answered.

And that was enough.

Would Solomon have been disappointed without riches or a long life? Would David have been any less a man after God's own heart if he'd been unable to form a complete sentence?

Again, no. These men, too, were pouring their hearts into the holy with no expectation except that God was passing by their lives and they didn't want to miss Him. And He heard them. And He answered.

And that was enough.

You're standing on the side of the road and God is about to pass by your life. You've got just one chance, one brief moment, to take your right-now heart to your right-now Savior and be heard. Do you want to waste that hiding in a heart of harbored hopes and holy words?

Then stop trying to pray like Solomon or David. Stop agonizing over holy or righteous words. Stop trying to sound more noble than you are. You're a nobody; you're an anybody, and that's fine. Those are the only people God has ever answered.

Straight-up pray when God gives you that moment.

Cry out with every ounce of your being from your honest heart, with all its hurt and its heaviness and its profound unholiness and its inarticulation.

Cry out honest, simple words.

And He will hear you.

And He will answer.

And if God only ever gives you the fullness of His mercy, isn't that enough?

## \ The Implausible Dream /

By the way, Solomon's famous prayer for wisdom, that prayer that resulted in abundantly more, that prayer that inspires us to try a righteous ruse, was not actually a prayer at all.

It was a dream.

"In Gibeon the Lord appeared to Solomon in a dream at night," the story begins in 1 Kings 3:5.

Then comes the meat with which we're more familiar.

"He said, 'What can I give you?' Solomon responded, 'You've shown great love to my father David, who was your servant. He lived in your presence with truth, righteousness, and commitment. And you continued to show him your great love by giving him a son to sit on his throne today. Lord my God, although I'm young and inexperienced, you've made me king in place of my father David. I'm among your people whom you have chosen. They are too numerous to count or record. Give me a heart that listens so that I can judge your people and tell the difference between good and evil. After all, who can judge this great people of yours?'

"The Lord was pleased that Solomon asked for this. God replied, 'You've asked for this and not for a long life, or riches for yourself, or the death of your enemies. Instead, you've asked for understanding so that you can do what is right. [wisdom] So I'm going to do what you've asked. I'm giving you a wise and understanding heart so that there will never be anyone like you. I'm also giving you what you haven't asked for – riches and honor

– so that no other king will be like you as long as you live. And if you follow me and obey my laws and commands as your father David did, then I will also give you a long life.'" (v. 5b-14, brackets mine)

Lest we've forgotten by this point, the writer reminds us of the illusion. "Solomon woke up and realized it had been a dream." (v. 15a)

It was only a dream. The question, then, is what will Solomon do with the dream once he's awakened?

He could have snapped his fingers and said, "Darn it! That would have been so cool!" and gone about his day, forgetting his dream but still sort of holding onto it in the hopes that maybe one day, it might come true.

He could have gone right back after it in his waking hours, falling to his knees beside his bed and begging for the wisdom he was convinced – until his eyes opened – that God had already given him.

He could have sought out a seer, someone gifted by God to uncover the meaning of the dream. Every other dream preserved for us is prophecy and cryptic to the point that it must be interpreted. Bundles of grain. Stars in the sky. Baskets of bread. Clusters of grapes. A giant tree. A tall statue. Cows. Each held a hidden message that only a man of God could reveal. Solomon could have looked for such a man of God who would know what this wisdom thing meant. What was God trying to say to me, he could have wondered?

But Solomon didn't need to wonder. He woke from that dream – I always imagine it was one of those very realistic dreams and that he arose with a smile he couldn't fully explain – and embraced every word of his prayer and God's answer. He lived like the dream was alive.

"He went to Jerusalem and stood in front of the ark of the Lord's promise. He sacrificed burnt offerings and

## The Implausible Dream

fellowship offerings and held a banquet for all his officials." (1 Kings 3:15b-c)

He went to the temple to thank God for the gift, offering burnt offerings – a sign of submission to God - and fellowship offerings – an offering of thanks. He woke up, submitted to the God He knew he'd heard, offered thanks for God's incredible answer, then ruled Israel as a man of wisdom.

And his wisdom was renowned. People traveled miles, months, even, for a chance to hear his wisdom. They came to ask him questions, to lay their issues before him, to find his answers because they knew him as a man of wisdom that came only from God. Never again was such a generous gift given as the one given to Solomon by the Queen of Sheba when she came to discover his wisdom and found it to be true. In fact, she said the rumors of his wisdom were not even half of it. (1 Kings 10)

Even today, when we talk about Solomon, we talk about his wisdom. Although we're obsessed with everything from the risqué to the outright crude, even though we can't get enough of *Sex and the City* or *Californication*, we don't talk about Solomon, the evocative lover who wrote the racy, raunchy, almost pornographic love poem that is also Scripture (Song of Solomon or Song of Songs). No, we talk about his wisdom.

All because he woke up one morning and took God at His word.

Solomon didn't stumble because those words were a dream. He had prayed and God had answered. He didn't need to be awake for that to be truth.

But the answer awakened him.

*pray*

There are many among us who might have awakened not encouraged, but discouraged. There are those who would have risen and wondered why we are never so bold in asking and why God never answers us that way "for real."

There are many among us who never would have lived wisdom because the answer was a dream. That's a shame.

But an equal shame is that there are also many among us who have heard God answer just as clearly when we've prayed with eyes wide open only to live like it was a dream and still not take Him at His word.

> The wild intoxication of God's yes fades into spiritual hangover as we sink into believing it must have been a hoax.

We have been told that God will answer us, but we never expect Him to actually come. We have dared to hope for greater things, but it is beyond our wildest imagination that God would ever grant them. We have all of these aspirations, these inklings, these ideas about good gifts, but it's hard to believe God is actually giving us these very things. We have dreamed of a God who hears our prayer and responds with a resounding, "Yes!" but when we hear that yes echo in the hollow of our hearts, we pinch ourselves and wonder if this is real.

Then we look in the mirror and know there must have been some mistake. We must not be hearing correctly. He couldn't be telling *us* yes, as weak and unworthy and unqualified as we are. The wild intoxication of God's yes fades into spiritual hangover as we sink into believing it must have been a hoax. This yes is so far-fetched that it could not possibly have been God.

## The Implausible Dream

In religious terminology, we call this discernment. In practice, it is no such holy thing.

We get this idea from verses like Mark 13:21-22 – "At that time don't believe anyone who tells you, 'Here is the Messiah!' or 'There he is!' False messiahs and false prophets will appear. They will work miraculous signs and do wonderful things to deceive, if possible, those whom God has chosen." Then we don't believe anything because every good thing must be a false prophet, every yes is no more than one of these deceptively wonderful things.

Or we read Proverbs 14:12 – "There is a way that seems right to a person, but eventually it ends in death" – and become wary of taking any path at all.

Under the guise of such "discernment," though it sounds holy enough, we're living unholy, static lives in which we never embrace the yes of Jesus because we're too busy dissecting the answer and if it doesn't seem plausible, we conclude it can't be God.

Do you think it sounded plausible to Solomon that he could ever be wise? This was a man praying for wisdom in his dream because maybe he was too timid to speak the words aloud. This was a man burdened with the kingship of a nation – and not just any nation, the nation of God's people – who was feeling wholly inadequate for the job. He wasn't praying for wisdom so that he could be the kind of king who would impress people. He was praying for wisdom because he didn't think he had it in him.

Do you think he really thought God would tell him that he did?

Yet Solomon never thought it wasn't wisdom. He never thought it wasn't God. He knew it was both and started living the dream.

If we want to live our dream, we must realize that God *is* implausible. He often answers as we least expect. He often says yes when what we're praying is "I'm not sure." He often blesses us with the very thing we least think we could ever have or transforms us into that which we least think we could ever be.

That answer – that blessing - is often somewhere between asleep and awake. It germinates in the honest prayer we would speak if our hearts weren't so inhibited by our consciousness – honest words like Solomon dared utter in his dream. Embracing his inadequacies. Confronting his inferiority. Addressing his insecurity. Asking for wisdom.

Then it is fulfilled in the courage to live like we've heard every word God has spoken, even when those words don't seem to make sense. Even when it's implausible. Even when our full consciousness takes over and says, "That can't be." Even when it seems like - or perhaps we even know - it has been a dream.

Part of honest prayer is pouring out our hearts unencumbered, undistorted. But the other part of honest prayer is living like a people answered.

A people who have heard God speak and determine to live as He's answered. A people who pray with hearts wide open, expecting Him to respond. A people who admit we've been sleeping; a people awakened by His word.

His resounding yes that seems so implausible.

We must be a people living the dream.

## \ Pray Today /

We are a people deceived by time and buried in excuses. We believe there is a perfect hour to pray, a good time to take our hearts before the Lord, and that good and perfect time is "later." We forsake this moment for the next one, trusting it will come and it will be better suited for prayer than now.

Trusting it will be a moment with fewer distractions. A moment of better clarity. A moment of greater quiet and stillness. A moment of stronger focus. A moment with better words and better energy and better discipline than now, the heat of the moment.

In the heat of the moment, prayer seems impractical. In any given circumstance, there are things we could be doing, steps we could be taking, a difference we could be making with our hands. Why would we fold those hands in prayer when we could put them practical use? We're not a desperate people; we are an innovative people. We can come up with something better than a frantic cry for holy help.

We'll pray later; now is the time for action.

In the heat of the moment, prayer seems impulsive. It reeks of desperation. As if we are a people who have forgotten how to fight, or a people who believe we shouldn't have to. It makes us seem like a people who can't handle even the tiniest setback, who aren't doing anything to help ourselves. Praying now seems like we're giving in. Praying now feels like we're giving up.

There is a word missing there, and literally, "it" changes everything. Being a people who drop to our knees does not mean we're giving up; it means we're giving *it* up. To a Higher power, to Someone more qualified to handle it.

This doesn't weaken us to fight; it strengthens us.

Consider the husband who calls 911 when his wife goes into labor in the kitchen. His instinct is to call in help, to get someone coming who knows what they are doing because he's fully aware he has no clue. He's still alone – no one just drops in to help him – but until help arrives, he has hope. There is a voice on the other end of the line to walk him through this. Step-by-step, a calming presence, a knowledgeable guide to get him through. More often than not, paramedics arrive to find these men in the kitchen floor with one arm around their wives and the other cradling their newborns, tears in their eyes and endless words of thankfulness pouring from their mouths. All because in the heat of the moment, they knew they were in over their heads and called for backup.

> Our now prayer isn't our quitting; it is our equipping.

That is the essence of "now" prayer. It's not that God is going to suddenly appear and take care of things. It's not that He's going to take away the necessity of our getting involved and doing something. It's not that He takes away the work of our hands or the things we would do to help ourselves. Our now prayer isn't our quitting; it is our equipping.

It is an invitation to another voice, a guiding force who knows what He's doing, to step in and bring us through.

And it is an invitation to thankfulness because we know we never could have done that alone.

*pray*

Now prayer is honest prayer. It is a sober assessment of a situation and our acknowledgement that we weren't made for this, followed by an invitation for God to make us more. Now prayer doesn't leave room for us to assess our words or worry about our posture or take notes on how the prayer is going; we can only cry out. That makes now prayer a powerful prayer.

But there is only power in now prayer if it is also expecting a now answer. Most of us don't pray with such expectation anymore. Jaded by the times we have fallen to our knees in now prayer only to have to handle the situation anyway, we struggle to believe God is ever coming now. Discouraged by the times when it seems God has waited, we only pray half a prayer.

Come, Lord, we pray, when what we really want to pray is, "Come now!" We settle for a simple "come" and figure God will get around to it. When He is able. In His good and perfect timing. When it's not so pressing as this very moment, but there's a little more space for a little more God. When we're not so frantic that we wouldn't see Him if He did show up.

Come, Lord. Later this afternoon, if You want.

Or tomorrow.

We love to give God until tomorrow.

We aren't the only ones. Prayers for tomorrow are common in God's story.

When Pharaoh's fields were flipping with frogs, Pharaoh begged Moses and Aaron to pray to the Lord to stop the plague. Moses agreed and asked Pharaoh, "When?" To which Pharaoh replied, "Pray for me tomorrow." (Exodus 8:10)

Tomorrow? What about the frogs today?

Tomorrow is also a prominent theme throughout the battles of the Old Testament. Israel's military leaders and prophets encouraged the troops by enticing them with tomorrow. Tonight, we rest; tomorrow, the Lord will hand the enemy over to us. All we have to do is wake up and walk over there.

Tomorrow? Is there some reason the Lord can't fight today?

We pray for tomorrow when we need God today.

The harsh truth is that if we don't believe in the God of today, we don't have a prayer for tomorrow.

*pray*

There are five reasons we pray for tomorrow.

*Tomorrow is good because it gives us the rest of today.* It gives us another few minutes or hours to try to figure things out, to consult our own experts, to search our own wisdom. It gives us another short time to gain new strength, muster our energies, and try to figure out some measure of good for ourselves before we have to surrender and admit our good isn't great.

> **If we don't believe in the God of today, we don't have a prayer for tomorrow.**

*Tomorrow is good because we've exhausted today.* By the time we finally cave in and submit to prayer – too often our last resort – we are worn down, flat-out exhausted and out of time and energy to do any more with that particular problem at this particular time. Or we have other things pressing in on us, tasks to accomplish, events to attend, things to do and we can't waste another second on this. With tomorrow's fresh energies, we'll be ready for whatever God's planned to deal with the problem.

*Tomorrow is good because we don't seem so demanding.* We don't want God to think we have no patience, that we can't handle a little trial every now and then. By building some time into our prayer, a little cushion, we aren't bothering God with every little trouble, not pestering Him to set aside all else for the sake of a measly us. We're letting God take His time so that we're not an inconvenience. Maybe He wasn't ready for this.

We know we weren't.

*Tomorrow is good because we can sacrifice today.* We don't want to miss a whatever lesson God might be teaching through the hard times. We've been taught that every moment is a teachable moment, every circumstance is a lesson in the making. So we give today to the teaching and pray for tomorrow's peace.

*Tomorrow is good because we have no earthly idea what we would do if we prayed and God showed up – just like that.* If God simply can come, and does, we tremble under the incredible power of a today God.

There are certainly more, but these are five of the primary reasons we pray for tomorrow - to give ourselves another chance, to wait for a better time, to acknowledge our place, to defer to God's wisdom, to shield ourselves from the raw power of God.

These are the reasons characters in our Bible stories were content to wait for tomorrow.

Pharaoh wasn't asking for tomorrow because he slept better to the chorus of croaking or because he was hoping with a little more time, the frogs might control some grand Egyptian insect problem. (Although they may have come in handy in the third, fourth, and eighth plagues had he thought to keep a few around.)

He was asking for tomorrow because he wanted the rest of today. He wanted to evaluate the problem, to investigate its scope, to talk to the top minds in his cabinet and see if there was any other solution to the problem, something they could do to take control of the situation themselves.

And he was asking for tomorrow because he was terrified to see God show up today. If by one simple prayer, this man Moses could bring his God to eradicate an entire population of frogs that likely outnumbered the entire population of Egyptians, then what other powerful word had this Moses spoken that Pharaoh had ignored? What powerful God had he dared to deny?

The leaders of the troops weren't waiting for tomorrow because God circled that date on the combat calendar or because they'd stumbled upon a fortified place to camp for the night. They were in the middle of the void, fully exposed to the forces they were about to invade. Not the best strategic move.

They were waiting because they didn't really have a battle plan; they were still evaluating the enemy. They were waiting because they were looking at a ragged band of soldiers who had already traveled all day and were too exhausted to fight all night.

> God didn't need tomorrow. ...He'd been there every day. He was there that day. He wasn't going to just show up tomorrow.

A tomorrow God renewed their energies. They would wake up rested, and they would wake up stronger because at dawn, God would be with them. The men would have felt invincible under the guidance of tomorrow God and would have fought with undefeatable vigor. The very idea that God would be with them tomorrow was enough of a reason to wait.

God didn't need tomorrow. He had told them to go. He was leading them one foreign people at a time to a promised land of milk and honey. He'd been there every day. He was there that day. He wasn't going to just show up tomorrow.

Their tomorrow was for them.

*pray*

James cautions us about relying too much on tomorrow. "You don't know what will happen tomorrow," he says in 4:14. Other translations say that we can't even know whether tomorrow is coming.

The only thing we know for sure about tomorrow and later is that if they come, they will be today and now. The God before us then will be earlier's later and yesterday's tomorrow, but He will be today's now.

Thank Heavens. Because we are a people who need God now.

We need His guiding voice, His encouraging strength. We need His comforting presence. We need the fullness of His power, the richness of His mercy, the gift of His grace and we need them now. We need Him now.

Which is why we pray for today. It may not seem like the perfect time, but there's never a better one.

Because tomorrow's never coming; it will always be today.

## \ Pray Out Loud /

Prayer, by our definition, has devolved into a time of quiet reflection and silent solicitation. When we say we're going to pray, we shut down. Heads drop, hands fold, and feet sort of scuffle in an awkward silence while we tick away the seconds in our heads until we can lift our eyes again.

Silence seems holy, but this prayer is missing something. Something vital.

That something is our voice.

The characters in our Bible prayed their personal, intimate, and desperate prayers with the full range of emotion of their voice, so much so that we can almost hear them when we read their words.

We hear the voice of Moses, crying out to a God whose goodness is questioned throughout the community. "By your great love, please forgive these people's sins..." Moses prays in Numbers 14:19, and we hear the repentance in his voice.

We hear the joy in Mary's magnificat, the way her voice sort of bubbles up and down in a prayer of praise. "My soul praises the Lord's greatness! My spirit finds its joy in God, my Savior...." (Luke 1:46-47)

From a prayer that is a psalm to a psalm of prayer - we hear the sobering humility of the psalmist as he prays, "Be kind to me so that I may live and hold onto your word. Uncover my eyes so that I may see..." (119:17-18a) And we hear the agony of a blind man seizing his healing moment. "Son of David, have mercy on me!" (Mark 10:48b)

The excruciating burden of the Cross comes through Christ's voice as He prays in the Garden, "Father, if it's possible, let this cup of suffering be taken away from me." (Matthew 26:39b)

Can you hear them? These are voices crying out, out loud.

In these voices, we hear the authenticity of the heart. We hear the honest ache of a thirsty spirit. We hear absolute faith even amid the questions. We hear questions in the face of absolute faith.

We hear the very things we long to hear in our own prayer. They are already there, in our every prayer. But they are not in the stillness of our spirits; they are in the boldness of our voice.

We have to dare to pray out loud.

*pray*

Something happens when we say the words.

It's one thing to think you believe in God; it's another thing entirely to say the words. When you say out loud that you believe in God, you hear what it sounds like to believe in God. You hear the doubt or the confidence in your voice. You understand where your heart is because your voice trembles in uncertainty, quivers in expectation.

Praying out loud also keeps us from obsessing too much about the ritual. When our prayers are untouchable, when they take place only in our minds, it is easy to edit and revise and revisit everything we did, everything we thought, every step we took to get to the place where we thought we had a prayer. We can go back to that thought practice and analyze what it was that we did, the wrong paths we took and the thoughts we corrected and the things we changed on our way to a polished prayer so that we can perhaps replicate our result.

When we pray out loud, there is no time for hesitation. In the quiet of the heart, we are prone to starting over for the sake of getting it right. Speaking out loud, we afford ourselves no such luxury. None of us bow before the throne of God and begin to pray, only to ask for a do-over somewhere before the amen.

"I got that wrong, Lord. Let me start over. Dear Lord…." Never. Praying out loud makes us commit to our words unedited in a way that a silent prayer never will. Unedited words of honest prayer.

And when we pray out loud, we remember having prayed. Praying out loud gives us the confidence of a sensory experience. There becomes something almost tangible in our prayer, something we can hold onto. It's hard to remember tomorrow or the next day or the next year what you once upon a time thought in a moment of quiet prayer; it's hard to remember the exchange that took place between you and God when it was all a matter of the mind.

When we pray out loud, we don't have to question whether we prayed or just thought about praying, whether we ever got around to giving our words to God. Our confession, our confidence, our doubt, our faith, our frustration, our honest heart echoes in our own voice and we remember that we said the words. In this one moment, we said the words and it's not what we said or how we said it or how long it took us to say it or how holy we sounded or any of that other stuff that we remember. We remember being physically present in prayer with the words of our mouth, speaking out loud the thoughts of our heart, and laying them down in the open space between ourselves and God.

We remember is that for that moment, we spoke and somebody heard.

*pray*

It's not always possible, we argue, to pray out loud. Some times are not the time; some places are not the place.

It might be socially inappropriate. There are quiet moments, sober times, hallowed places where even a quiet voice would interrupt another man's peace.

By all means, respect those around you. Honor the people, places, and times that would be shattered by an uttered prayer. But understand how truly few and far between these times and places are.

Far more often, it might be socially questionable to pray out loud. There are persons who would be offended by our audible of faith.

Someone may always be offended when we pray. We can't let that stop us. Jesus never did. Nor did any of the men and women who came to Him. A bleeding woman, an unclean woman, pushed through the crowds. Blind men screamed from the side of the road. A paralytic dropped through the ceiling of another man's home. A sinful woman walked into a religious man's house, dropped to her knees and poured expensive perfume all over Christ's feet. People were offended. That never stopped anyone from going after God.

That never stopped God from coming to them. He ate in the sinner's home, welcomed children onto His lap. Jesus was offensive; the Gospel still is. That's no reason to hesitate. We cannot defer to a world that doesn't want to listen when there is a God who is waiting to hear our voice.

## Pray Out Loud

Praying out loud might be socially awkward. Someone might hear us praying and wonder who we are talking to. They might even think we're crazy.

In these days of mobile connectivity and Bluetooth technology, almost everybody is talking to somebody that nobody else can see. Nobody's crazy any more; just connected. So go ahead and make the connection with the God who doesn't need an earpiece to hear you. Don't be shy about it. The girl in the elevator isn't.

But no one should hear us pray, we argue. That is in the Bible somewhere.

That verse is Matthew 6:5-6:

*When you pray, don't be like hypocrites. They like to stand in synagogues and on street corners to pray so that everyone can see them. I can guarantee this truth: That will be their only reward. When you pray, go to your room and close the door. Pray privately to your Father who is with you. Your Father sees what you do in private. He will reward you.*

> We cannot defer to a world that doesn't want to listen when there is a God who is waiting to hear our voice.

We are not hypocrites, so we cannot pray out loud.

But that's not what Jesus says. Jesus does not say, "Do not ever let anyone hear you pray." That would be nonsense. It is through the prayers of others that we have learned to pray at all.

The Scriptures are full of the prayers of God's people – men and women across the generations who prayed out loud and who, because of their willingness to share their hearts, have taught us how to pray.

Imagine if they hadn't. Imagine if throughout the Bible, we kept running across this word "pray" but we never saw any example of anyone actually doing it. The word would be nonsense. We would read "pray" the same way we would read "porgen" or "azigmo." It would be gobbledygook. It would be this weird, cultish, cryptic practice that we knew the people of God engaged in, but which we could not describe, let alone "pray" ourselves.

There would be no guidance, no standard, nothing to explain to us the mysteries of prayer, which are that we can talk to God, that God does hear us when we pray, that it doesn't take a special formula or ritual, and that we ought to just talk to God like we'd talk to our neighbor or our family or our friend. That it is ok – more than that, that it is prayer – to simply talk to God.

It is because these men and women shared their prayers, because they prayed out loud, that we know how to pray at all. (And because they did such a good job of it that we never think we are praying well.)

The heart of this verse in Matthew is not, "Do not let anyone hear you pray," but instead, "Do not pray for their sake." Do not pray because you are heard by man; pray because you are heard by God. Do not pray because someone might hear you; pray because God does. Do not go searching for the best place for your voice to carry; carry your voice to God.

The men that Jesus was speaking against – the Pharisees, the hypocrites – weren't praying on those street corners. They were shouting. They were shouting holy-sounding, righteous-sounding words without considering the God who heard them. The words that they "prayed," in the loosest definition of the term, were not words that were heavy on their heart. They were not questions for which they were seeking answers. They were not burdens they were asking God to lift.

They weren't actually asking God for anything. They weren't thanking Him for anything. They weren't praising

Him for anything. These "prayers" had nothing to do with God.

They weren't really prayers.

*pray*

When we engage in honest prayer, we don't worry about being hypocrites. We don't worry about who might be within earshot. We don't worry whether this is a street corner or the corner of the closet. We don't worry whether this is the time or the place.

Because any place where we let our hearts cry out to God is the place and any time we risk to put our words in our voice is the time.

It is the place and the time to seek our God. If in the moment we so happen to cry out, there so happens to be someone nearby, then so happens. Our prayer is meant for Him and for the sake of the One who hears us, we pray.

We are focused on God. Pure and simple.

So pray in honest prayer. Speak your honest heart.

Speak your aching heart. Speak your thankful heart. Speak your fearful heart. Speak your wondering heart. Speak your wandering heart. Speak it out loud.

Pray out loud and let your heart hear your words. Pray out loud and put a tangible energy into your prayer. Pray out loud and let the echoes of faith resonate within you. Pray out loud and know what it feels like to speak His name.

Prayer is not about a moment of quiet reflection; prayer is about having a voice before our God.

You have a voice. Use it.

## \ Pray Drunk /

In the toughest of times, simple prayer doesn't seem like enough. It doesn't seem simple prayer does justice to our burden. In the toughest of times, it's not enough to "just" pray. So with aching hearts, we "pray really hard."

Pray really hard, as if our average everyday prayer is somehow substandard to this moment. Pray really hard, as if the words we had been saying could never be enough. Pray really hard, as if God hears us better when we theatrically carry our worries to Him. As if God hears us better when we strain and struggle and burden ourselves with prayer.

And that's what we do. We burden ourselves with our prayer. Because it's a stage play, a show, and nothing more. Because we have to memorize our lines and our cues, come in on time and hold just the right amount of dramatic effect. It's our painstaking attempt at hopefully getting prayer "right." It's a skit we're putting on for the sake of our Father, who hears us anyway, as we try to convince Him to listen because this is the big one. This is *the* prayer. This time, hear us, Lord.

We believe there are levels of prayer. There are dynamics of conversation that indicate the significance, at least to us, of what we are asking. We pray softer prayers of thanksgiving, quiet words of humility. A little bit louder prayers of bitterness or anguish, frantic prayers for healing. Our loudest prayers are those for the things we really want. Or think we want.

If we pray a little louder, a little longer, a little more charismatically, then God will understand that we really want this and may even be fooled, as our hearts have been fooled, into thinking that we need it.

It's because the prayers in the Bible seem so dramatic. They seem somehow better than what we would dare to pray. We get caught up in how big these prayers seem – the vulnerability, the emotion, the pleading, the agonizing – and we think that we, too, must pray a grand prayer if we ever hope for God to hear us.

But these Biblical prayers are not dramatic prayers. Not to God. These are not better prayers. These are simply honest prayers, and the lesson we should take form them is not to pray really hard but to really pray our hearts.

*pray*

A woman named Hannah arrives at the temple, desperate to bear a child. Her husband's other wife has borne many children, and she fears his love is at stake. She was angry at God for her barren womb, and at the sacrifice in Shiloh, she prayed her heart. 1 Samuel 1 tells us she was in tears as she prayed.

"Lord of Armies, if you will look at my misery, remember me, and give me a boy, then I will give him to you for as long as he lives. A razor will never be used on his head." (v. 11)

There's one way to read Hannah's prayer, and there is another way entirely to read Hannah's prayer. We might read it with the same agony we can imagine praying it, the same dramatic show we might put on had we been in Hannah's shoes. The same self-aware tears, the same whispered question of whether or not He's hearing us or if we should pray harder. The same manipulative tone that is desperate to make sure this is a good prayer, or at least will be an answered prayer, as if our tone has any bearing on such things.

That is not how we should envision Hannah's prayer. Because that's not how Hannah prayed. Back to the story:

"While Hannah was praying a long time in front of the Lord, Eli was watching her mouth. She was praying silently. Her voice couldn't be heard; only her lips were moving. Eli thought she was drunk." (v. 12-13)

Here is this barren woman, this resentful and fearful and broken woman, kneeling at the altar of God and praying her most desperate prayer, praying "really hard," yet not in a voice that is meant to be heard. She's putting no agony in her voice, no pretense in her posture. She's praying. She's forming the words. But it's not from her mouth that she wishes to be heard; it is from her heart.

And she is so moved by emotion, so honest in her heart, that she comes off intoxicated to Eli, the priest in Shiloh and a man who has certainly seen many a prayer. Maybe even many a drunken prayer. He believes Hannah is drunk as she seemingly rambles before the Lord, pouring her heart out at the altar.

> When we want to pray really hard, we pray really long.

"For a long time," 1 Samuel says, which is another characteristic we often attribute to praying really hard. When we want to pray really hard, we pray really long.

We see that in Hannah's story, and it must run in the family because later in the same book, her prophet son, Samuel, is shown doing the same thing.

"Samuel was angry, and he prayed to the Lord all night." (15:11b)

Samuel was angry enough to pray all night, and so we might guess that means he was praying really hard. He wanted to make sure God was hearing this, that God was hearing him. He wanted God to know how angry – and how dedicated to his anger – that he was, so he prayed all night!

That may be our reading, but that's not why Samuel prayed instead of slept. He prayed all night because the next morning, he was going to come face-to-face with Saul and he didn't know what to say to the man. He was angry with the king but Samuel understood that his anger, even righteous anger, got him nowhere. There is no word of God in the prophet's anger; he needed a better word. He prayed until he heard a better word.

Then there is Jesus, who prayed in the garden with Roman soldiers approaching. The Son of God Himself prayed not once, not twice, but three times for the cup of suffering to be taken from Him. That is certainly a "pray really hard" moment if ever there was one – that moment just before a righteous man was betrayed.

It looks to us like Jesus was praying really hard, but He was just praying urgently. He was praying an agonized heart with every second that He had to pray, knowing His time was coming.

These stories are our evidence that there must be such a thing as praying really hard.

We think, like Hannah, we must make a spectacle of it, that we must appear out of character, or at least, out of place. That our agony must be painted on our faces, if not carried in our voices.

We think, like Samuel, we must pray long. We must deny ourselves simple graces, like sleep, and pray all night to prove that we really mean it.

We think, like Jesus, we must pray often, back to back to back if necessary. We must continue to walk away, to seek a solemn space, and to ask again and again and again until it's too late to ask any more, until the Romans are standing at our gate.

That is what we think when we read these prayers, but that should not be the takeaway. None of these are what it means to pray "really hard," if even there is such a thing. These are lessons only in how to pray at all.

*pray*

From Hannah, we learn what it means to pray with fullness of emotion. Not created or contrived emotion, but the honest pleadings of an aching heart. When you feel like there's something worth praying "really hard" about, pray like Hannah in fullness. Throw yourself into your heart and work your way back out through prayer. Pray with such raw, honest emotion that anyone watching might mistake you for drunk.

What is drunk? Drunk is having lost all inhibition. Drunk is having lost respect for all protocol. Drunk is making a scene without being conscious of making a scene. It is saying what is on your mind without cleaning up your language, sorting out your thoughts, or necessarily making full sense.

> [Drunk] simply is what it is and refuses to be ashamed of itself, and it is a powerful way to pray.

Drunk disregards ritual and discards propriety and goes full-tilt after whatever it wants however it can figure out to get there. It simply is what it is and refuses to be ashamed of itself, and it is a powerful way to pray.

From Samuel, we learn what it means to pray ourselves empty. He prayed to pour out his anger so that it could not eat away at the very heart with which he talked to God. He prayed all night not so that God would hear him but so that he had space for God to enter back in. He prayed so that when he went to meet Saul, he would have something worthy to say. A word from God and not from anger. He prayed until he could hear that word; it just happened to take all night.

Truthfully, God couldn't care less how long (or short) our prayer is, so long as we say and hear every word we need to and not a syllable more. He is not impressed by a longer prayer any more than a shorter one. In fact, He warns against praying long prayers in Matthew. "When you pray," Jesus says in the Sermon on the Mount, "don't ramble like heathens who think they'll be heard if they talk a lot. Don't be like them. Your father knows what you need before you ask him." (6:7-8)

Heathens! Heathens, God says, pray long prayers thinking that's what it takes to be heard. Heathens, He says, ramble on and on and on until they think their prayer has been long enough. Heathens, God points out, pray "really hard." Heathens, Jesus teaches, should not be your role model for prayer. They pray thinking God hasn't heard them, but the truth is that He knew before they asked.

He knows what you need before you ask. He also knows what you want and how badly you want it before you say a word. He knows how your heart is aching for this answer or how it is tormented over that question. He knows how you've convinced yourself that this is the thing that changes everything. He knows how you believe that this is the big one. It doesn't take a production to tell Him that. He's not impressed by your long-windedness or your dramatic effect. Such things only become a burden to you.

They are a burden because they draw you away from the very prayer you want to offer. They are a burden because they make you think more about the prayer you're offering than why you are offering it. They are a burden because they bury you in ritual and weigh you down with getting it right. They are a burden because they make you think more about the words you say and how you say them than the word He longs for you to hear.

That word is, "I hear you." That word is, "I know."

From Jesus, we learn what it means to keep coming back, to pray again and again while there's still time. We pray urgently because the time is coming.

The time is coming when the guards are standing at the gate and it's do or die. The time is coming when we have to make a choice, when life takes its course, when whatever is about to happen is happening. The time is coming when there won't be time to pray, so pray while you can, as often as you can, until that time comes. Because that time is coming.

*pray*

This is what it means to pray "really hard." It isn't scripting a performance worthy of an Oscar. It's not moaning and whining and wailing in the contorted agony of our hearts. It's not being intimidated and pressured by what seem like bigger prayers in the Bible.

We pray really hard by praying without inhibitions. We pray really hard by emptying ourselves before the Lord. We pray really hard by praying often, knowing the time is coming.

This is honest prayer. Nothing more and nothing less. These seem like bigger things when Hannah or Samuel or Jesus do them, particularly when God also answers them, but these aren't bigger things; these are simple things. Simple, honest prayers.

These simple, honest prayers show us that in the toughest of times when we feel like we ought to be praying really hard, when a simple prayer doesn't seem like enough, it is enough.

The key to praying really hard…is simply to pray.

## \ Pray Continually /

Instead of saying Jesus prayed often in the garden, we might say He prayed continually, as Paul instructed the church at Thessalonika to do. "Pray continually," he told them in 1 Thessalonians 5:17. Another version says "Pray without ceasing." Yet another says "Never stop praying."

These are words we stumble over. Tough orders, we think, to pray all the time. We try to encourage ourselves by relenting that not all of our prayer has to be formal. We can pray regardless of what else we are doing at any given moment. We can pray in our cars while commuting to work. Pray in the checkout line at the grocery store. Pray while watching television. Ok, at least during commercials.

We talk ourselves into thinking that maybe we can do this. Maybe we can pray every second. Maybe we can pray without ceasing. Maybe if we focus hard enough and discipline ourselves well, we can never stop praying, not even to catch our breath.

Then inevitably, we skip a beat, miss a moment, and come down hard on ourselves for failing in even this. If we cannot keep this line of communication open with God, if we cannot keep the dialogue going, if we are not in constant prayer as God, through Paul, has told us to do, then we have failed. We are unworthy pray-ers. And then comes the internal struggle about whether any prayer matters if we do not constantly pray.

Take heart. Paul doesn't tell us to pray continuously. Read it again. He only tells us to pray continually.

Continually means to come back to something again and again and again. It is not the same as continuously, which means forever and ever and ever.

He doesn't tell us to pray without stopping. He tells us, look again, to pray without ceasing.

Ceasing means giving in and pulling back. It is not the same as taking a break or taking a breath.

Even what we've translated as "Never stop praying" is not an order to never pause praying.

Stopping means giving up and walking away. It is not the same as pausing.

The Greek word Paul uses here is *adialeiptos* (ἀδιαλείπτως), which translates as, "with no unnecessary gaps in time." An alternate definition is "as frequent as necessary." Or yet again, "regularly, yet intermittent." Yet another definition says *adialeiptos* "refers to what happens *regularly*, without implying '*always*' or '*uninterruptedly.*'"[1]

Paul's words, then, do not mean, "Pray always and forever." What Paul says to the Thessalonians and to you and to me is, "Pray again and again and again. Do not give in and pull back. Do not give up and walk away."

What Paul says is "Pray as often as you have to."

As often as you have to for what?

That depends. What is the purpose of prayer?

If we concede that prayer is not about getting everything we want or even necessarily everything we need and that instead, prayer is about the relationship between us and our God, then the ultimate purpose of prayer is to be heard by and to hear from God.

If that much is true, then when Paul says to pray as often as you have to, what he is really saying is to pray until you know you've been heard. And pray until you hear.

*pray*

Sometimes, that means we pray words we prayed before. Words that still weigh heavy on our hearts. And that is ok. There is nothing wrong with using old words. Jesus prayed three times in the Garden, each time using similar words. David repeats the same phrases again and again in the Psalms.

In Psalm 3, he cries out to God because his enemies are after him. In Psalm 18, he prays again because again, his enemies have been after him. In Psalm 35, he begs the Lord's help against those who are coming against him. Psalm 40 is another prayer for rescue from the hands of those who pursue him.

Need we continue?

David doesn't pray again because he thinks God has not heard him. No. In fact, David repeatedly praises God for hearing him. He prays again because the trouble is fresh in his heart and he wants to be heard. Again. He wants the reassurance that God is still listening, that God still hears him, even though his heart and his faith assure him this is true.

He prays again because, like all of us, David simply wants to know that his God has not forgotten him. Whether or not his enemies turn back.

You can't help but notice while reading through the Psalms that so many seem to say the same thing: rescue me, Lord; help me, Lord; heal me, Lord; praise the Lord. Every few chapters, David cycles back to an old theme and prays again, often a mix of new words and old words. Words that resonated with him from an old prayer and words fresh in his heart for the new one.

We keep coming across these go-to words, these repeated phrases. And when we hit them the second time, the third time, the fourth time, we start thinking, "Didn't I already read this? Wasn't this another Psalm? Didn't David already pray these words?" And we think somebody somewhere had to double copy some lost piece of parchment, that someone missed the memo that this particular prayer was already in there.

But no. These are recycled words, not recycled prayers. David chose these words because something about them stuck with him. Something that contented him when circumstance circled back around. When he found himself facing the same situation again, he remember these simple words he'd once prayed in a moment and the peace that washed over him when he formed them with his lips. The peace he'd felt when he remembered how God had heard them.

He used these words as a starting point for a new prayer, a place to pick up the conversation again. A place to engage his heart that, let's be honest, maybe wasn't into prayer at the moment. When the same troubles keep coming back at you and you remember how powerfully you've prayed over them, it's hard to think of praying again. It's hard to know where to start when what you've already prayed seems so good and yet, so ineffective.

You start with old words. You start with words you remember hearing God hear, not so that He would hear them again but so that you would. So that you would remember tangibly, physically, fully what it was to be heard. So that you can go after a new prayer with the same passion for hearing from the God who has heard you, the same hunger for the peace of knowing He has heard.

You start with those words that are still how you feel, but you surround them with new heart. You surround them with new passion, with new hunger, with new exasperation as the situation so dictates. You take this powerful moment you once had, this powerful prayer encounter that you can't seem to forget, and you surround it with the new moment to create a new prayer.

A prayer that you've never prayed before, even though it sort of feels that way.

*pray*

We are too easily deterred by prayers that sound like ones we've already prayed. We hear ourselves using similar words, taking a similar posture, crying out of a similar heart and we recognize that prayer. Sadly, we let that stop us.

We hear our old prayer falling into our folded hands, and we are discouraged. What's the point? we wonder. Didn't I just pray this?

We prayed. We prayed this prayer and nothing happened. We prayed and nothing changed. We prayed and here we are again, praying over the same thing when it's fairly obvious that prayer is not going to work.

In our distress, we turn to one another and throw up our hands. I don't know what to do, we tell our friends. They ask us if we've prayed about it.

Yeah, I've prayed about it, we answer. But nothing. I prayed and nothing happened. That was my chance, and I blew it.

That was God's chance, and He blew it.

And our friends shrug like that's all they've got, too. That's the best they had to offer and well, if you already prayed and that didn't work, then nobody knows what to tell you.

Paul knows what to tell you. Paul tells you to pray again.

Odd words to a people like us. A people who think we have one shot at prayer, one chance to pray about something and then it's over. A people who have become so hurried and so busied and so averse to prolonged discomfort that we can't imagine praying and waiting and praying and waiting and praying again.

A people so distrusting of God that we've come to believe if He doesn't answer right away, He will never answer at all.

A people who still believe the answer is fulfillment of desire. A people who still believe the answer is that our good and gracious God gives us what we're seeking. Ask, He says, and it will be given unto you. (Matthew 7:7) We're asking. God's not giving. Either prayer doesn't work or we're not doing it right.

> God doesn't want to hear how right we get it.

That's why it is easy to fall into a constricted, contrived ritual prayer. We believe we have just one chance at prayer, one chance at an answer, and if there is no answer – if we don't get what we wanted - then we didn't get it right.

God doesn't want to hear how right we get it.

He wants to hear how deeply in our heart our longing echoes. He wants to hear how emptily we hunger for Him. He wants to hear how desperately we rely on Him. He wants to hear how firmly we believe in Him. He wants to hear how honestly we trust Him. He wants to hear how confidently we run to Him.

He hears these things when we pray continually. When we pray again and again and again. When we keep coming back to our knees to talk to Him one more time.

We pray continually, and God gets to hear us. He gets to know our hearts. He gets to see our faith. He gets to hold our hopes.

We pray continually, and we get to hear our God. We get to hear His heart. We get to hear His grace. We get to hear His mercy.

To be heard by and to hear our God – this is the essence of prayer.

*pray*

The perpetual pray-er David knew that.

In Psalm 3, with the enemies attacking, David has the peace to say, "But you, O Lord, are a shield that surrounds me. You are my glory. You hold my head high. I call aloud to the Lord and he answers me from his holy mountain" (v. 3-4) just before he continues, "Arise, O Lord! Save me, O my God!" (v. 7a). His enemies haven't retreated when He declares the Lord his glory; he declares the Lord his glory when he knows the Lord has heard.

In Psalm 18, recalling his imminent destruction, he turns to praise in saying, "I called on the Lord in my distress. I cried to my God for help. He heard my voice from his temple, and my cry for help reached his ears." (v. 6) He goes on to say that "the earth shook and quaked. Even the foundations of the mountains trembled. They shook violently because he was angry." (v. 7) He continues for many verses about the anger of the Lord.

Not the Lord who came down and destroyed his enemies; that Lord comes later. This is simply the Lord who heard him. Who heard David's desperate cries and responded with His own emotion. David praises *that* God before he even mentions the God who saves him.

Why?

Because not even David wanted a God who gave him everything he thought he wanted.

Nobody puts their faith in a God of the magic lamp, who is just a rub or a ritual prayer away. Nobody puts their hope in a Holy Father controlled or manipulated by His child.

We put our faith in a God who is greater than that. We believe in a God who is wiser than that. We place our hope in the God who is more than we might make Him to be, the God who simply is.

The God who simply hears us.

He is the God we hear crying back to us, *Child, I hear you. And I'm happy when you're happy, sad when you're sad, angry when you're angry, hurt when you're hurt. I'm even angry when you're hurt. My nostrils flare with smoke and raging fire comes from My mouth.* (Psalm 18:8)

*I hear you, child. And I want to hear from you.*

*Again and again and again.*

*Over and over and over.*

*Pray as often as you need so that you know that I hear you.*

*Please, child, never stop praying. Never stop talking to Me.*

And we won't.

Because we are children of a good and gracious God who hears us, we will pray. And pray. And pray again.

And because we are children of a good and gracious God from whom we need to hear, we will pray continually.

# \ Paradoxology /

Prayer is not always easy. There are times in our lives when it is easier to fall than to fall to our knees. Situations where it is easier to lie down than to lay our burdens down. Days when we would rather give up than give it up to Him. Moments when we close our eyes, drop our heads, and there is simply darkness.

That's life.

That's holding a mound of bills in one hand and a dwindling balance in the other and measuring the contrast of a God who said He was steady with a life that is anything but.

That's holding your wife's barren belly and longing for a child of your own that the doctor says is never coming, and remembering a God you used to call Father while wondering if you will ever know what that means.

That's holding the hand of a loved one as their last breath fades, and thinking of a God who raised the dead but who seems painfully absent in this hospital, in this room, in this moment.

In these trying times, it is hard to pray.

We feel down and out. Weary. We are weak, worn down. We can't lift another finger. We just can't do it any more. We feel so alone.

There's no one out there looking for us. No one to help us up. No one who even noticed we have fallen. We are nothing in the sight of this world, and when we look in the mirror, we are nothing there, too.

Depression, defeat, and exhaustion weigh us down. There's no point in getting up. No point in climbing out.

No point in praying.

Not to a God who seems to have abandoned us. Not when we are surrounded by trouble with no hope to hold onto. Not in a desert with no merciful rains coming. Not to a God we're starting to question. Not to a God we aren't sure any more exists.

Surrounded by a world that doesn't seem to know us, we are supposed to believe our God does? And in a world that can't hear us, how do we believe that God can?

Rejected, dejected, the last thing we want to do is take that final leap into crazy and be *that* person. That person that looks desperate. The one that talks, out loud, to nothing at all and only hopes there might be a God and that He might be listening.

We wonder if we ever knew Him, if He ever knew us. If the Bible is simply just a story. If He has our best interest at heart or if the non-believing world is right and He is a distant, dispassionate, or worse – sadistic - God.

> We are supposed to be pouring out our hearts, but we can't even feel them any more.

We are supposed to be pouring out our hearts, but we can't even feel them any more. We are crushed under the weight of a heavy burden that seems impossible to bear. We are ready to give up, but we feel like we have to let go of nothing or everything.

Through all of these questions, we are supposed to pray?

In the depths of darkness, in the deepest of pain, when there's no energy left even to blink and we are questioning the very nature of God Himself and the last thing we want to do is pray, yes. That is what He tells us to do.

Pray anyway.
And praise Him.
Consider it a paradoxology.

*pray*

A doxology is praise we offer to God. Literally, from the Greek, it is a "word of glory."

In common practice, the doxology comes at the end. It is the last few words of a prayer, the last stanza of a poem, the final verse of a song. The praise is the final word, leaving a sound of honor lingering in the air and a word of love to echo in your heart. When we offer a prayer of praise with the last of our energies, the tail end of our breath, it is doxology.

One of the most well-known doxologies is one we sing in many of our churches, or once upon a time, we did. Page 48 in the church hymnal, if you were sitting in my pew. Simply called "Doxology," the song was a single verse meant to be sung in closing or in a quiet time of reflection.

Perhaps you remember these words:

*Praise God from Whom all blessings flow. Praise Him all people here below. Praise Him above, ye heavenly host. Praise Father, Son, and Holy Ghost. Amen.*[1]

These are simple words, nothing extravagant. But they bring our hearts back to a praise-worthy God, with all of creation, above and below, praising Him in the Trinity.

Doxology is the refocusing. It is turning around and making sure that at the end of it all, we remember who God is and we praise Him for being.

In the Lord's Prayer, we use doxology as the opportunity to turn a situation back to God, ending in surrender, acknowledging His supremacy. "For yours is the kingdom, the power, and the glory forever. Amen."

Those words are not part of the original prayer recorded in Matthew 6:13. They were added later as the final note, the sticking point, the doxology. Instead of saying come, do, give, forgive, and deliver us, Lord, goodbye, we have added these words to acknowledge His Lordship over the Kingdom: It is Yours, Lord. Forever.

That's doxology.

And in that Kingdom, our God is a God of paradoxes. That is, He is the God of things that seem to be contradictory but in truth are actuality.

God says to be first, you must be last. To be greater, you must be lesser. To be the leader, you must follow. To be the bigger man, you must make yourself smaller. To be raised up, you must humble yourself. To be anything, you must be nothing.

These are paradoxes – that in order to be what you'd seek to be, you must become exactly the opposite.

So it serves to follow that when you pray, when you praise and honor God when it seems there's nothing to thank Him for, you are engaging in the paradoxology.

The paradoxology stems both from our faith and our hope. It is our prayer to a God we can sometimes only faintly remember, trusting that if He was present with us once, He will certainly be again. It is our prayer to a long-lost Friend who says He hasn't changed.

It is our prayer that God is who He says He is, who He has shown Himself to be. That He turns our downs to ups and transforms our valleys to mountaintop experiences. That when we are weak, He makes us strong. Because we aren't going to get strong on our own. We haven't the energy or the means. And we've usually, by now, tried; it wasn't working.

## Paradoxology

It is our prayer that when we are last, He puts us first. That when we have nothing, we have everything.

That when we seem forgotten, He remembers us.

Because He is.

The paradoxology praises the contradiction in our God. We praise Him for being counterintuitive, for being contrary, and for challenging conventional "wisdom" with the Promise of the truly Wise.

*pray*

The pages of our Bibles are filled with the faithful who understood the paradoxology. They knew the same depression, the same struggle, the same internal battles we know and faced the same temptation to turn inward rather than out, but they also knew what we often forget – they knew the God of the paradox. Knowing Him, they did not merely resort to prayer; they sought it. When they had little breath and tired eyes, these men and women turned first to prayer.

> The paradoxology praises the contradiction in our God.

Elijah collapsed under a broom plant and waited to die. He prayed surrender in desperation.

David hid in the back of the cave with Saul and his men out front looking for the anointed wee one. He prayed protection in fear.

Daniel was a captive in Babylon. He prayed integrity in bondage. Shadrach, Meshach, and Abednego were in a furnace. They prayed salvation in fire.

Joseph sat naked in a cistern. He prayed righteousness in vulnerability.

Mordecai was marching to the gallows. He prayed vindication in betrayal.

Jonah was in a whale. He prayed in a whale!

These men knew hardship. They knew the tough times. They knew the challenge of thinking of God when it didn't seem He was thinking of them.

Yet each of these men is known for his righteousness. And in these dark moments, each was known for his prayer. These men turned to God when it wasn't easy. They may not have known how God would show up, but they prayed anyway, and they praised Him. Because they knew Him as the God of the paradox.

Elijah praised Him as the omnipotent God, all powerful in a moment when the prophet felt empty.

David praised Him as the God of the shield and Lord of the Armies, a fierce warrior for the sake of His children. He didn't have to lift a finger.

Daniel praised Him as the God of freedom. Shadrach, Meshach, and Abednego praised Him as the God who walked beside them.

Joseph praised Him as the God of compassion, a God who clothed him in righteousness and raised him to honor.

Mordecai praised Him as the God who turned the tables, hanging a man in his own noose.

Jonah praised Him as the God of second chances, who pursues and uses you even after the world has chewed you up and spit you out.

These men knew the trouble they were up against, but they knew the contradiction, too. They knew the nature of the God to whom they prayed.

*pray*

## Paradoxology

When we know the true nature of the God who hears us, it becomes easier to turn to Him in prayer. It becomes easier to seek Him first, not to beg for mercy but to offer praise.

We praise Him because He is greater and He is wiser and He is contrary to whatever we think we're about to succumb to.

Once we submit ourselves to the countercultural and counterintuitive life of one who trusts fully in God, we find our hearts wrapped in the paradox. It not only teases and entices us; this holy paradox defines us.

God wraps us in His arms, and we have never felt more loved. Or more unworthy of that love. We are defined by graciousness.

He holds us in His comfort, and we have never felt more secure. Or insecure. We are defined by confidence.

He guides us in His wisdom, and we have never felt more certain. Or more profoundly aware of our naiveté. We are defined by perspective.

He enables us in His strength, and we have never felt more capable. Or more weak. We are defined by courage.

He centers and defines our lives, and we have never felt more humbled and grounded. Or more unrealistic. More aware that we're living beyond the impossible into the improbable of a life that could exist if only it couldn't.

> **It not only teases and entices us; this holy paradox defines us.**

It is a dream, a fantasy, and yet we are living it. We are living the paradox, and it defines us. And it defines for us a relationship with our Father, our God. He is the Masterful Creator and the God of the Paradox.

And for that, we praise Him.

The paradoxology.

The paradoxology praises Him because He says when you are weak, you are strong. Praises Him because He says when you are last, you are first. Praises Him because He says when you feel lesser, you are greater. Praises Him because He promised when you're down, He will raise you up.

And you praise Him because, despite your best efforts, you could only have one or the other on your own accord. You would either be weak or you would be strong. And whatever you have would be only a half-measure at best.

Praise Him because through Him, you gain a full measure of both. A knowledge of Him and perspective on yourself. Knowing what He is to what you're not and how the beautiful interplay of the two of you creates something dynamic that matters to His story and yours.

Praise Him for being contrary. For being counterintuitive. For being the God by which when you empty yourself for His sake, you are filled to overflowing with the power of the God of the paradox.

Even when it's easier simply to fall, fall to your knees and praise Him. Pray the paradoxology.

## \ Pray Unconditionally /

Maybe one of the reasons we fold our hands when we pray is because we are haunted by their emptiness. As we come again before the throne of God asking for yet another saving grace, we know we have nothing to offer (or have offered nothing) in return. As much as we like the idea of a God who could give, give, give, it offends our sensibilities if we take, take, take.

So we fold our hands to mask their emptiness, bow our heads, and bargain with the God of the Universe just to feel like we are offering something.

If You do, Lord, then I will.

If You help me out of this situation, Lord, then I promise I'll go back to church.

If You heal me or heal my loved one, God, then I promise I will serve others.

If You find me the funds to make this month's payments, Jesus, then I will turn off my television and choose worship instead.

If You give me one more chance to make this right, Father, then I will wake up every morning and read my Bible first thing.

If You come right now, God, and answer the aching of my crying heart, then I will never ask for anything again.

Conditional prayer is not honest prayer. Even if you *really* intend to go back to church and serve others and turn off the television and read your Bible. Even if you *never* ask for anything again, which, by the way, is a term God would never agree to.

The promise to go away is not an offering to God; it's an offense. When you promise never to ask for anything again, what you're actually saying is that this one thing – this one particular thing that might seem to satisfy you in this one particular moment – is more important, more powerful, and more fulfilling than a continuing relationship with the God of the Universe, your Creator, and your Father. That doesn't honor God; it cheapens Him. Just as those other conditional prayers cheapen church, cheapen service, cheapen worship, and cheapen His Word.

Whatever we offer in exchange for God's favor is cheap.

That's not what God wants. God wants us to live in richest blessing. He's not waiting on us to come up with the right trade-in or sign on the dotted line. He's just waiting on us to come. Come with honest asking. Seek His face, plead for His voice. Lay our hearts out before Him, asking for our needs and yes, even our wants.

We don't have to bargain for God's promised mercies.

We just have to ask.

*pray*

But God is a conditional God, you might argue, citing any of a number of times God's promise is embedded in an if-then statement of His own.

"If you carefully obey me and are faithful to the terms of my promise, then out of all the nations you will be my own special possession," He says to Israel in Exodus 19:5.

"'Bring one-tenth of your income into the storehouses so that there may be food in my house. Test me in this way,' says the Lord of Armies in Malachi 3:10. 'See if I won't open the windows of heaven for you and flood you with blessings.'"

"If you forgive the failures of others, your heavenly Father will also forgive you," Jesus preaches in Matthew 6:14.

"If you obey my commandments, you will live in my love," our Lord continues in John 15:10.

Even His greatest promise contains this if-then. God so loved the world that He gave His one and only Son, that *if* we believe in Him, *then* we shall inherit eternal life. (John 3:16)

These are only five of more than two hundred of God's promises wrapped in a stated or implied if-then in the Bible, through His words and the words given through His prophets.

If God's promises to us are conditional, then why can't we pray a conditional prayer?

Because we could never accept the terms. Look at the fine print:

Jacob bartered. "'If God will be with me and will watch over me on my trip and give me food to eat and clothes to wear, and if I return safely to my father's home, then the Lord will be my God,'" he declared in Genesis 28:20.

Seven chapters later, Jacob returns to his father's home in time to see Isaac die. The next time we hear about Jacob, we hear the story of his jealous sons selling his favorite son Joseph into slavery, then lying to Jacob about Joseph's fate. Is this what God as Lord looks like? The very next word about Jacob after his barter is fulfilled – after by his word, the Lord became his God - is the story of him losing his son and buying the lie that Joseph has died.

Compare that to a God who declares "I AM the Lord," then loses His Son to a jealous world but refuses to believe the death is the end.

Jephthah negotiated. "'If you will really hand Ammon over to me, then whatever comes out of the doors of my house to meet me when I return safely from Ammon will belong to the Lord. I will sacrifice it as a burnt offering,'" he offered in Judges 11:30-31.

Jephthah defeated Ammon, with the Lord's help, and returned home to find his daughter running out the doors of his house to meet him. He tore his clothes in grief and made a new deal with her: She had two months to roam the mountains and mourn, and then he would fulfill his deal with God. When she returned, he sacrificed her as a burnt offering before she had grown up, married, or given him a grandchild. He sacrificed more than his daughter; he gave up who knows how many future generations for such a measly prize as Ammon.

Compare this to a God who foresaw what His offering would be and did not sell His Son short. He gave His Son the fullness of life and an incredible work of ministry, both knowing the sacrifice they were working toward. Then He gave His Son for a greater prize than Ammon; He gave His Son for the return of Creation itself.

Hannah haggled. "'Lord of Armies, if you will look at my misery, remember me, and give me a boy, then I will give him to you for as long as he lives,'" she offered in 1 Samuel 1:11.

The Lord of Armies answered her prayer and gave her a son. She named him Samuel, and after weaning him, she returned him to the temple and dedicated him to the Lord. But she never stopped thinking about him. The continuing story tells us that every year, Hannah made a

## Pray Unconditionally

new robe for Samuel and took it to him during the annual festival. She did her best, but she could not wholly let go of her son.

Compare this to a God who turned His back on His Son in one agonizing, heart-wrenching moment in which He fully surrendered Christ to the reformation of the temple.

Three examples of men and women praying conditional prayers to God with their own terms in mind. But God's counteroffer is always the same: it will cost you your child. Whatever you're asking for, whatever you think you can offer Me in exchange for My favor, will come down to this: Will you give Me your child?

> Whatever you're asking for...will come down to this: Will you give Me your child? Because I'm giving you Mine.

Because I'm giving you Mine.

This essentially takes our offer off the table. It's a price we cannot pay. We cannot, even in the best of intentions, give our child in the same way that God gave His. We would give up, hold out, and hold on just as Jacob, Jephthah, and Hannah did. We cannot hold up our end of the bargain with the same fullness as any promise of God, so we are not in a position to be making deals.

Not because God holds His child against us. He was both willing and pleased to offer His Son. But Jesus takes our terms off the table.

*pray*

God's not into bargaining. Not for what we could offer Him and not for what He offers us. Although His promises are wrapped in these if-then statements, these are not conditional terms. He does not once say, "If you honor me, then I guess I will be God." Instead, He lays out the logic of our relationship – that if we, as fallen people, put everything we've got into being His people, we will reap the rewards of that relationship.

If we faithfully keep to the terms of His promise, then we will be His treasured possession. (Exodus 19:5) What do you do with your own treasured possessions? Of course, you display them so that anyone who sees will know what matters to you and what that looks like. God is saying, if we are faithful to Him, we become His people on display. We will be people who demonstrate what it means to move beyond created and into loved by this beautiful relationship we share with Him. Everyone who sees the way we live in this love will know what matters to Him and see what faith and promise look like.

If we bring one-tenth (a tithe) to His storehouses, He will open the windows of Heaven for us. (Malachi 3:10) No longer bound by what looks like bounty on earth, we will find a new awareness of our "more than enough" when the windows of Heaven open and show us where our true treasure is stored. Unburdened and unattached to all that is here, we are free to see through God's window what truly is – Heaven.

If we forgive the failures of others, God will forgive our failings. (Matthew 6:14) It is not that God withholds His forgiveness until we forgive; it is that we do not understand or appreciate the depth of His mercy until we have lavished that mercy on others. We are forgiven already, but it is not until we forgive others that we *feel* what forgiven means. The forgiveness of God takes on new meaning and we live forgiven from the heart instead of merely the word.

## Pray Unconditionally

If we obey His commandments, we will live in His love. (John 15:10) We were created to live in His love, but disobedience in the act known as the Fall separated us from that when man suddenly felt like he had a reason to hide. Obeying His commandments removes from us this guilt, this shame, this shortcoming that tells us we need to run away from God. It frees us to walk the world with Him, living in His presence and companionship - and love - as He originally intended because we are living as He commanded us to live.

If we believe in Him, we will inherit eternal life. (John 3:16) An inheritance is gained not after the death of the heir, but at the death of the benefactor. Eternity isn't waiting for us to leave this life for that one; eternity is now. Christ died on the cross and left us eternity. When we believe that, we are freed from this culture of death that we call life and begin truly to live.

> God being God does not depend on what we do or do not do.

God being God does not depend on what we do or do not do. God doesn't do anything *because* of our faithfulness, our obedience, our interpersonal relations, or any other thing that we do. He is God regardless. But these things that we do, these disciplines we exercise, allow us to experience the full glory of God, which is never conditional. It is always relational.

*pray*

There is one notable exception, and that is Eden. Eden was the one circumstance where what one man and one woman did or did not do had the potential to affect God's very design for Creation. This could change everything. And when it came to this, God didn't bury His grace in the seemingly conditional.

He never said, "If you eat the fruit of this tree, then you cannot be my people." He didn't say, "If you eat this fruit, we can't be friends any more." He never threatened, "If you have just one bite, I will kick out of this garden forever." He didn't tenderly warn, "If you eat the fruit of this tree, you will ruin everything."

No. When it came to this one situation that was truly conditional – this one unique circumstance where what man decided to do had a profound effect on the very dynamic between Creation and Creator – God didn't bother with a quippy little if-then statement. He flat-out said, "Don't do it." Do not eat the fruit of that tree.

For us, it's not about the fruit; it's about faith. It's not about Creation; it's our hearts on the line. It's not everything; it's our thing. We have to decide.

God's if defines our choice. His if tells us what love is, what love looks like, how love lives, so that when we choose to love or leave, we know what we're choosing.

If we choose love, we get the fullness of God, and He shows us what that looks like. It is a life as a treasured possession, overflowing with blessings and living in His love, looking through the windows of Heaven, forgiven and alive. (Or conversely, if we choose to leave, we get nothing of God. It is a life rejected, expelled and abandoned, burdened and guilty and condemned to die.)

God's if is not a threat. It's a promise. It's a promise that love is waiting for our hearts to choose.

Our if is not a promise. It's a threat. It's an ultimatum that God's only going to get from us what He's willing to give and He's got to give first.

God isn't threatened. He's neither intimidated nor impressed by our barter. He's heartbroken.

## Pray Unconditionally

The only condition that God is interested in is the condition of our hearts.

And Job says "if you want to set your heart right, then pray to Him." (11:13)

Not barter. Not bargain. Not negotiate. Not deal.

Just pray.

Unconditionally.

# \ Thy Will Be Done /

Prayer is not a barter, but neither is it a resignation. Too many of us treat prayer like nothing more than the opportunity to speak at our sentencing hearing.

*Just do what You're about to do, God. I'm nothing more than a guilty man. You're the judge for a reason; let's get this over with. Thy will be done.*

*Thy will be done*, we repeat again in resounding resignation as we turn our heads, hide our hearts, and wait for whatever God's plan might be.

God's plan. That divine, cosmic, completely-out-of-our-control, once-upon-an-eternity hope we hold out that this is for the best and one day, it will make sense.

We shoulder the burden of circumstance instead of carrying it to the Cross in search of our Savior because we have been storied and sermoned to death – literally to death, as so many of our stories and sermons are wrong - about God's plan.

God has a plan, we've been told. His plan is greater than our plan. His plan is wise. His plan is non-negotiable. And it doesn't have to make sense. He doesn't owe us an explanation for His plan.

But we owe Him our expectation.

That's what we tell ourselves, that even in the toughest times, we are supposed to expect the best of God because He has a plan. We are supposed to believe, as Romans tells us, that He's working everything together for good. We are supposed to stand with Paul and rejoice in our suffering. These times, even these trying times, are part of the plan. This is God's will.

So we take life's lumps and craft a lesser prayer. Help us endure this time, this trial, Lord, we pray. And let us learn whatever it is we are supposed to be learning.

Thy will be done.

We climb to our feet defeated, trying not to step on any holy toes. Trying not to ruin this imperfect moment in God's perfect plan.

Prayer is not meant to be defeating. When we rise from our knees more burdened than we fell, that is not God's will. That's not part of the plan.

God's plan is that His people would come to Him. It is that we would humble, but not diminish, ourselves before Him. It is that we would cry out.

God's will is that we would pray and give Him space in our hearts, not dominion over them.

*pray*

*Thy will be done* is a phrase we see in the prayer of Jesus, which is why we think this is a good way to pray.

When He taught the disciples and the crowds to pray, He included, "Thy Will Be Done." (Matthew 6:10)

We read those words resigned, knowing the painful surrender required to put our plans in His hands. We read those words and hear Jesus telling us to give up all personal hope in deference to God's grander plan. We read those words as though they are the only ones in this instructional prayer.

But they're not.

*Thy will be done* in the Lord's prayer is not the only word; it is one of *thirteen* phrases Jesus spoke. It is part of the conversation, not the entirety of it. It is one surrender amid many others, one measure of give in a give-and-take, one calling forth in a back-and-forth.

Broken down, we see the interplay of reverence and deference, solicitation and surrender in Jesus' prayer.

*Our Father in Heaven.* This is reverence, acknowledging His name and place.

*Hallowed be Your name.* Deference. We are turning the attention on Him.

*Thy Kingdom come.* Solicitation. We are asking Him to make Himself present.

*Thy will be done on earth as it is in Heaven.* Here is our phrase, fourth in the prayer. It is deference, giving Him this place and reverence, recognizing His Heaven.

*Give us today our daily bread.* Another solicitation, asking for the fulfillment of our needs.

*And forgive our trespasses.* Solicitation again, requesting His mercies.

*As we forgive others.* Surrender. We are giving up our grudge to honor His gift.

*Lead us not into temptation.* Surrender and solicitation, giving up on finding our own way and asking Him to show us His.

*But deliver us from evil.* Solicitation, begging for His rescue.

*For Yours is the Kingdom.* Surrender, giving Him ownership of His Kingdom.

*And the power and the glory.* Deference, recognizing His awesome nature.

*Forever.*

*Amen.*

This is not a resigned prayer. This is not a defeated prayer. This is a crying out. It is a conversation starter:

Lord, You hear me and I need You here in the fullness of Your goodness because I'm hungry, I'm guilty, I'm lost, and I'm persecuted and I don't know what to do about any of it. But You know what You're doing, Lord.

You're wonderfully good, and I know that. That's why I want You here, doing what You do. Being God.

Contained in our amen is the concession that we wouldn't have it any other way.

That is the essence of the Lord's Prayer. It is a dialogue. But we read these words and walk away with just four of them, a resigned *Thy will be done.*

What happened to the other fifty-five words?

*Thy will be done,* whenever we see it in Scripture, is always just one part of a bigger prayer. Never do we see a man praying, "Dear Lord, Thy will be done. Amen." It's never the whole thing. Often, it's not even the main thing.

Look at the prayer of Jesus in the garden.

The disciples are sleeping, and Jesus wanders off to pray. He knows what awaits Him at the Passover. He's about to become the Lamb, and He's understandably a little hesitant about the whole plan.

> But we read these words and walk away with just four of them, a resigned *Thy will be done.*

Which is interesting because Jesus knows the whole plan! He's been in on it from the very beginning. He knows the wisdom and the power with which God is about to shake the world. He knows more fully than any of us could ever imagine exactly what is about to happen.

Yet even He won't settle for a simple surrender. Even He won't give in to *Thy will be done.*

He doesn't walk into the garden, fall to His knees, and resign Himself to the plan, even the plan He already knows is incredible, immeasurable, and good.

No. He tells God what He's really thinking. "I don't want to do this. This isn't my idea of a good time. This is going to hurt. It's going to break everything inside of me. I'm really not looking forward to this, and if there's any way to change the plan, now would be a great time to do it. I know the plan, Father. I get what You're doing here. But I'm not thrilled about it. I don't know about my own ability to be a sacrifice. So whaddya' say? Think we can bypass this whole Calvary thing? If not, I understand because I know what we have been working toward. (Thy will and not mine, Father) I know You are my joy and my strength. I know You are with me. I know You are here."

Jesus doesn't want to do it! He knows the plan. He knows the outcome. He knows the glory and the grace and the absolute goodness that is about to come. He knows God's will and He *still*, in His flesh, tells His Father what He thinks about the whole thing.

Before He adds, *Thy will be done.*

He speaks His heart first and then surrenders. When you think about the relative peace with which Jesus carries His cross, know that it started in the garden. He wasn't resigned but rejuvenated by a powerful prayer about God's plan.

Is it any wonder we have no peace? We, unlike Jesus, do not know the plan. We don't get it; we don't understand it. Yet we wholly resign ourselves to it with four defeating words. We pray *Thy will be done* not as a part of our prayer but as the entirety of it. Or worse, as the culminating negation of it.

But we see in Jesus, in the very prayers that teach us *Thy will be done*, that this is never more than half a prayer and it never diminishes any other honest word we pray.

When we put *Thy will* in its place as just a part of our prayer and never the whole, we create space in which God can work. Between our preference and His plan, we lay bare a place for His presence.

And He comes bearing the gift of peace.

*pray*

Job is a man who needed peace. Although righteous, his life was crumbling around him. And his friends were less than encouraging.

They bought in to the must-be-God's-will principle and exhausted themselves trying to convince Job there was nothing he could do. All his petitioning and prayer and demanding of God was not going to matter because God did these sorts of things to men at His perfect discretion. If Job was in a pile of ashes, it was because God wanted him there and put him there. His friends kept pushing him to give up his crying out and just accept God's "will."

Job would have none of that. He persisted in his honest prayers. Admitting he didn't get it. Admitting he didn't know. Admitting he wasn't happy about the horrendous circumstances that were coming to define his life. Owning his grief. Owning his questions. Owning his heart and pouring it out before God.

He wasn't trying to change God's will, if that's what he was facing; he was trying to understand it. He wanted to know how his experience was working in God's story and what God was doing through him, if anything at all.

He was praying for an answer to a question that is only asked in honest prayer - he wanted to know if he mattered. He wanted to know if he was still part of the plan, even if he wasn't particularly enjoying this part of it. He wanted to know if there even was a plan.

Job cried out. In response, God showed him the miniscule traits within each living being, what makes a giraffe a giraffe or why the ostrich has wings.

## Thy Will Be Done

God answered Job with a glimpse of the small and seemingly unimportant because He knew that in that moment, Job felt small and unimportant. God answered Job's heart by pointing out all of the small things woven together in His creation with the greatest of care. This strengthened Job, and he understood God's love for him in even his smallest moments. He was reassured there was a method even in the madness.

Job refused to resign himself to something so vague as "God's will" and instead persisted in prayer. In return, he found peace for his questioning heart - God still heard him. God still answered. God still cared.

> We don't feel like co-authors of our own lives. We don't feel like precious, beloved children of a gracious God. We don't feel like people with a prayer. So it's no wonder we don't' feel like praying.

*pray*

The problem with *Thy will be done* is that when we resign ourselves to some grand scheme of God we can't understand, we have no peace. Like Job's friends, it's too easy to believe that the bad things in our life are part of God's will. We think He beat us up, broke us down, chipped us apart, and cracked us from our head to our toes. We think this is part of His plan.

How do we reconcile that with a God of love?

The discrepancy between the God we hope for and the God we are resigned to leaves us more confused, more discontented to pray. It adds to our defeatist posture. We are doubly defeated when we believe prayer is nothing more than an immediate resignation of any hope we ever had to a God who for some unknown, and unbelievable, reason works through destroying us.

We don't feel like co-authors of our own lives. We don't feel like precious, beloved children of a gracious God. We don't feel like people with a prayer.

So it's no wonder we don't feel like praying.

But *Thy will* is not what we've made it out to be. It is surrender, but it is not defeat. Prayer should never be defeating.

God's plan is not that we wait for His judgment; His plan is that we testify. His plan is that we pray. That we talk to Him, pour out our hearts, tell our side of the story.

His will is that we cry out.

Rather than praying, *Thy will be done,* as holy as those words may sound, the way to honor God in prayer is simply to do His will…and pray.

## \ Come /

When we cry out, what we often want is for God to get down here.

Down here where the world is a mess. Down here where there is pain, despair, agony. Down here where there are tears, heartache, and questions. Down here where we could really use a sense of Your presence, Lord.

From the pain in our hearts, we beg Him to come.

And He comes. Or should we say – He never left. From the foundation of the world, He walked among His people. Thousands of years later, He still walks among us. He still holds our hand. He still hears our cries, wipes our tears, dries our eyes. He still hunts for us in the bushes.

Yet in the grips of our pain, it's tough sometimes to find Him. That's why we so often pray, "Come, Lord."

There's nothing wrong with that. We need Him to be here. We need His comfort and His healing touch. We need His presence and His promise. And trapped as we are in these hearts and flesh of limited understanding, we need Him to come because that tangible presence is something we can almost comprehend.

In times of great trial when He stands beside us in the darkness and weaves Himself into the tapestry of our lives, we know He is here. It is peace that passes understanding. We can't explain the peace we see in the joy of the dying, the peace in the steps of the homeless, the peace in the hearts of the broken – but we get it.

It is God.

He loves loving us, standing beside us, walking with us, coming to be with us. He comes every time we call.

But God doesn't like spending time in our broken world any more than we do.

He doesn't relish living in our mess. He doesn't enjoy traipsing through our wilderness from one dark spot to another, just to show up and be God again when our hearts cry out in agony. He comes, because we ask Him to come. He stays, because we beg Him to stay. He loves, because He is love. And He doesn't begrudge us our flesh.

But listen closely, and you can almost hear Him crying back to us, "Is this all you'd have Me for?"

If all we ever see of Him is what He does when He shows up to answer us, we get an image of what God can do for us, but very little insight into who He is.

What does it teach us about God when He shows up after we've called? What do we learn when He comes yet again to stand beside us in this circumstance or that, heal this friend or that family member, open this new opportunity, close that old one, or any of the other million little things we're always asking Him to get down here and take care of?

> But listen closely, and you can almost hear Him crying back to us, "Is this all you'd have Me for?"

We learn that God is there to answer us. That His primary job is to hear and to answer and to make sure things are working out as we pray they would.

And when we believe His only job is to answer us, we start to paint Him into this box. Of rescuer. Of healer. Of completely personal supernatural force. Of magic genie.

That's why it's so easy to get angry with God when the unpredictable or – dare I say – the prayed-against happens. When cancer wins. When foreclosure wins. When divorce wins. When betrayal and despair and disaster win. It's easy to rail against God because we have heard, and believed, He was perched in Heaven just waiting to come down and answer us.

Of course, He's not that kind of God. But it's easy to think He is. After all, He continues to respond to our agonized prayers and emotional appeals and wannabe guilt trips that "If You were any kind of God…" or "If You loved me at all…" or our desperately whiny, "You promised!" with a stomp of our feet.

Why does He do it? Why does He let us think these tricks work? Why does He come?

Because He did promise. He promised to be here whenever we need Him, and whenever we call on Him, He promised to come. No matter how twisted we have our end of the covenant, God is not about to break His promise.

He doesn't wait for us to ask nicely. He doesn't wait for us to get the right words. He doesn't wait for us to assume the right posture or speak with an appropriate tone in our voice. He doesn't wait for us to consider the foolishness or wisdom of our asking. He simply comes.

He comes because what He hears is our heart crying out – COME! He comes because the rest of our prayer – even when it's short of being honest, even when it's an unveiled attempt at divine manipulation, even when it's a selling short of God and all that He is, not to mention us and all we are - falls away. In all those words, He hears only the one – Come!

So He comes. He'll work out the details when He gets here.

*pray*

What His coming does is two-fold. In an instant, it answers our hearts and teaches us something about God: He is trustworthy. He said He would be a friend and that He would come when we called Him. He is. And He does. By simply showing up, God shows Himself. Whether He answers as we expected or that sense of His presence just overwhelms us, when God shows up, we know. We know He is here. We know He is God.

More importantly, though, His coming gives Him a place to start whittling away at us, working in our hearts. He takes our invitation to be here as an invitation to start working, to pry away the layers that keep our hearts stuck in the shallow prayer of "Get here, God!" and to begin healing, hallowing, and sanctifying us by His presence.

This is the God we see showing up in the Bible. This is the God we see answering the prayers of men like Jeremiah, Jairus, and the tax collector.

Jeremiah was discouraged. He felt like the last righteous man struggling amid the success of the wicked. He was doing what he believed right in the Lord's eyes, and it was getting him nowhere. In distress, He cried out, "Come!" Come and justify me, Lord. Because I am right and this crazy, messed up world is completely backward.

Then God came and answered Him, saying, "I am here." I heard your cry, Jeremiah, and I have come. You need not worry about those wicked men; this is all the success they will ever know. I will take care of it. I'm going to set My judgment on those who defile my people and betray my name and gain by cheating. Count on it.

Jairus pursued Christ as his last hope to save his dying daughter. She was very sick, and this man followed along until his voice carried enough above the crowds to be heard. He begged, "Come!" Come and heal my daughter, Lord. Because I cannot bear to lose her.

## Come

Then God came; Jesus went, saying, "I am here." I hear the agony in your heart crying out, and I have plans for your daughter's life. I am coming to heal her.

The tax collector invited Jesus, "Come!" Have dinner with me and my friends. Sit in my living room; eat from my kitchen. Because nobody thinks there's more to me than my professional reputation, and I'm starting to believe them.

Then God came; Jesus went, saying, "I am here." You are not what you do. You can live an honest life, and I will stand by you and break bread at your table because you matter. Pass the rolls.

To each man, God came. He stood beside them. He announced His presence, and even His plan, but none of these men saw Him work as they had expected.

God didn't let His fury fly and actually bring about the destruction and judgment He told Jeremiah He was bringing. It didn't happen in that second; Jeremiah didn't get to see the powerful, instant wrath of God rain down on the wicked. Instead, God encouraged Jeremiah with just the word of His promise.

His presence made Jeremiah a better Jeremiah. Jeremiah learned to look beyond injustice and focus on God, content and faithful in waiting.

Jesus didn't make it to the little girl's bedside in time. He did not rescue Jairus' daughter from death. Jairus had to experience the heartache of losing her. Though the voices said it was no use for Jesus to come now, not since his daughter had died, Jesus continued to come to Jairus and to the little girl. When He arrived, He awakened the child.

His presence made Jairus a better Jairus. Jairus learned to look beyond the impossible and to have faith in a God that was bigger than he even imagined.

The Lord ate in the home of the tax collector, but He didn't hold a press conference about it. Jesus tasted the disgrace of living a tax collector's life and quietly put His reputation on the line to help the tax collector come out from under his.

His presence made the tax collector a better tax collector. The tax collector learned not to define himself by his role but to define his role by his integrity.

He came because they asked Him to come. But it was His presence — not His granting of their requests (because He didn't) — that was their answer.

His presence spoke to something deeper that their hearts did not have words for. Each man was convicted by the wisdom in the way God simply came, the way He used those moments to hallow them. They found new strength and a deepened faith as they saw what God wanted to do in them and through them, not just for them.

> He came because they asked Him to come. But it was His presence that was their answer.

The same is true with us, which is why God is so quick to come. In the presence of the God who comes, we find our questions fading. We are able to embrace His presence and defer to His wisdom, wait on His timing, see His plan.

This new perspective leads us to a new prayer. It is thirsty prayer. Honest prayer.

Honest prayer maybe starts with asking God to come here but ends with us begging Him to sweep us away. It opens our hearts, changes our lives, radicalizes our very existence in a powerful, indescribable, and undeniable transcendence of the confines of this world into the expanse of the holy. He comes to us, but honest prayer takes us to Him, in full realization that He wasn't created for this world; it was created for Him – for Love, for Mercy, and for Eternity.

*pray*

There was a lady at my church who was battling cancer. She was absolutely beloved by our congregation, and our hearts were heavy with her struggle. One Sunday, someone rose to lead a prayer on her behalf, and he said the words, "Lord, come be with her."

When you call God to the bedside, He is one more person in the room. He is a part of what's going on, but it's easy to lose Him as the central point of it all. (For the record, He came; He healed her.) A better prayer, though – a more earnest, honest, and longing prayer – would have instead cried, "Lord, let her rest in You."

One invites the Lord to be one of us; the other aches to be one with Him.

Isn't that what our hearts are truly crying? Lord, we want to be with You!

Our longing, even when we don't get the words quite right or we pray for something shallower, isn't lost on God. That's why as often as we pray, "come," He comes and answers, "you, come."

More often than we see characters in the Bible praying for God to come, we see Him inviting them. Come to the mountain. Come to the burning bush. Come walk with Me. Come fish with Me. Come here and look at this; isn't it cool? Come.

He wants us to come to Him. To be one with Him. To humble ourselves and to present ourselves before Him. Not to pray for Him to come down, but to pray for Him to raise us up. He wants us to pray for eternity.

Because a change in circumstance does not demonstrate the heart of God. Only a change in the heart can reveal His glory, His mercy, and His grace. His Love. And only a glimpse of eternity can change the heart.

It is the difference between knowing what God can do for you and knowing who God can be for you. Between inviting Him to touch your life and pleading to rest in His hand. Between demanding He speak and being still enough to hear the whisper.

It's one thing to see what God can do in the constraints of our earth-bound flesh – and He will come. Pray Him come.

But it is something entirely different to see what He can do beyond this place. To see God in His element, not in ours. To do that, we have to pray – in honest prayer - not for God to descend but to transcend our existence and take us somewhere.

Pray Him take us somewhere holy.

And He bids us, "Come."

# \ Healed /

When He comes, we want God to heal us, our broken bodies and our wounded hearts. We want this healing to be easy. And we want Him to be quick about it.

There is, by some argument, a Biblical precedent for this. We read the stories of holy healing in the Gospels, and the narrative tells us they were almost instantaneous.

*"Jesus told the man, 'Get up, pick up your cot, and walk.' The man immediately became well, picked up his cot, and walked."* (John 5:8-9) Immediately.

*"Jesus asked him, 'What do you want me to do for you?' The blind man said, 'Teacher, I want to see again.' Jesus told him, 'Go, your faith has made you well.' At once he could see again...."* (Mark 10:51-52) At once.

*"Then a woman came up behind Jesus and touched the edge of his clothes. ...When Jesus turned and saw her he said, 'Cheer up, daughter! Your faith has made you well.' At that very moment the woman became well.'* (Matthew 9:20, 22) At that very moment.

*"Jesus reached out, touched him, and said, 'I'm willing. So be clean!' Immediately, his skin disease went away and he was clean."* (Matthew 8:3) Immediately.

*"The man was possessed by demons and had not worn clothes for a long time. ...Jesus ordered the evil spirit to come out of the man. ...The demons begged Jesus to let them enter those pigs. So he let them do this. The demons came out of the man and went into the pigs. Then the herd rushed down the cliff into the lake and drowned. ...The people went to see what had happened. They came to Jesus and found the man from whom the demons had gone out. Dressed and in his right mind, he was sitting at Jesus' feet."* (Luke 8:27b,

29a, 32b-33, 35) Dressed and in his right mind. Just like that.

No wonder we believe in an almost instantaneous Jesus.

Almost instantaneous and virtually pain-free. He didn't run a laser through the blind man's eyes. He didn't scrape plaques of leprosy from the infected man's tender skin. He didn't cauterize the woman with the bleeding disorder. He never used a scalpel, never cut through a person's already-broken flesh. Jesus simply touched them – or they touched Him - and in many cases, not even that. Sometimes, He only spoke a word.

Almost instantaneous, virtually pain-free, and absolutely complete. The paralytic man did not stand up, work the cramps out of his atrophied legs, stretch for a few hours, stumble around, and then walk home. Luke says he stood up and walked away. Another translation says he "jumped up." The blind man did not stumble with half-squinted eyes; Mark says he saw. The demon-possessed man did not linger naked in the cemetery. In the time it took to walk to town and back, he'd found clothes and dressed himself. Their healing, their transformation, was full. These men and women were whole.

These stories leads us to believe in and pray to an immediate Jesus, an instantaneous, pain-free, complete healer of a Messiah. All these individuals had to do was get themselves to Jesus. *That* was the hard part. Tracking a Man without GPS, pushing through the throngs of people whose hearts were aching just as hard, getting a moment with the Rabbi's ear – this is all the burden they had to bear. The rest was easy Jesus.

But when we pray with one eye open, looking for the instantaneous, pain-free, complete healing of Christ, what we find is that it's not so simple. We come, we cry, we cry out. Then the chemo takes months. Apologies hurt. Infection festers. We have to daily swallow our pride and eat our words and break our spirits to get even a glimpse of the God passing by.

We want a quick fix in a holy moment, but it's never that easy. There's always a struggle. The Gospels make it look quick and painless, but they don't tell us the broken's side of the story.

*pxy*

The Gospel writers don't tell us how the paralytic groaned as he stretched his aching legs to stand. They don't tell us how the blind man closed his opened eyes to shield them from the sting of the sun. They don't tell us how the deaf man, the bleeding woman, the demon-possessed learned to live again.

Maybe, as we quickly believe, the healed didn't have to; maybe their healing was just that easy.

But maybe it wasn't, and the writers of these Gospels chose simply not to include those details because whatever they were, they were not part of the narrative. Whatever happened after Jesus spoke to, touched, and spat on these men and women was not part of His story.

> We want a quick fix in a holy moment, but it's never that easy.

His story is, "You are healed." End. Done. Finito. That is that. These writers – Matthew, Mark, Luke, and John – are trying to tell us not that the healing of Jesus is easy. Not that it's simple or painless or instantaneous. They're trying simply to tell us that it is. It simply is.

It is a wholly holy moment.

Men came to Jesus broken, and they walked away healed. Women came to Him aching, and they walked away restored. The details, as much as our wounded hearts two thousand years later may want to know, are not the story.

If we knew the particulars, if we found these men and women to have the same struggle with healing that we seem to have, if we knew that it hurt, that it took patience, that it took perseverance, that it took something from the broken in order to be healed, would we not miss the story of Jesus entirely?

We would put ourselves in the broken's shoes. We would read about what it took from the paralytic to walk again and would think him a courageous man. We would read about the blind man whose eyes stung with the brilliance of the world, and we'd think about how we've known times like that. We'd read about the woman with the issue of bleeding and focus on what it took for her to walk through the crowds like that. And we'd think her brave or crazy or both. We'd think about these men and women more than we'd think about this Man and that doesn't draw us into the Gospel; it drags us away.

To maintain the integrity of His story, we just don't get all the details. But because these stories were written by human hands, we do get a few notable reminders of the very raw experience of healing. The tough stuff, if you will. A couple of details that don't draw us away from what Jesus was doing yet encourage those of us struggling somewhere between broken and blessed.

Details in the form of a demon-possessed boy and a herd of pigs.

*pray*

The pigs were innocent bystanders at the miraculous healing of the demon-possessed man from Luke 8 that we read at the beginning of this chapter. The Legion of demons came out of the man, entered the pigs, and ran the whole herd of them off a cliff. Were it not for the pigs, don't think for one second that demon wasn't trying to take that man off the cliff. Because when the battle of two dominions meets in your flesh, there's no such thing as an easy surrender. I believe that as Jesus healed that man, those pigs spared him the tremendous pain of an exiting demon while reminding us in the way only God can that no healing comes easy; sometimes, you have to give up the bacon.

And just what was the pain of an exiting demon, besides plunging off a cliff? Ask the little boy in Mark 9. At Jesus' word, the demon comes out of him, but not before it throws this child into a violent convulsion, thrashing his body about one last time as it makes its exit. It nearly killed the boy; in fact, everyone thought he was dead. (v. 26) Neither the father nor the boy nor the onlooking crowds anticipated this; they thought that when Jesus said the word, the demon was gone. They thought it would be easy.

Healing was never easy. It never is.

An encounter with God when there is warring in your flesh is nothing simple. More often than not, it takes everything out of you. It always feels like it does.

Because we've wrapped our lives around our brokenness and lived to accommodate its burden. A blind man learns to feel his way through an unsighted world. A deaf man, to sense his way through silent space. A paralytic, to accept a friend's assistance. A wounded heart, to shield itself. A broken body, to respect its limitations. An aching spirit, to turn its back on belief.

Then Jesus comes along and restores us, and in our wholeness, we are emptied. The mechanisms we've developed to tolerate our pained places aren't necessary any more. What worked so beautifully yesterday doesn't work today. We have to wake up and figure out what our eyes are seeing, what our ears are hearing, what new truth has entered our bodies, our spirits, our hearts. And we have to figure out how to live with that.

There's the rub. There's the hard part. There's where it's easy to get lost in the details, get wrapped up in how we're supposed to handle healing when we know there's nothing to handle and yet, there is everything to change. There's where it's easy to lose the story.

The Gospels don't tell us this, but the demon-possessed boy probably battled a headache and fatigue. He probably walked around for the next day, the next week, the next years of his life with that weight of not knowing when those demons would come again, maybe still planning his life around the possibility that they could while desperately wanting to believe that they couldn't.

> What worked so beautifully yesterday doesn't work today.

The blind man probably kept his hands out in front of him, probably continued to feel around his world. He probably struggled to learn how to live sighted. Where he may never have considered he might be doing something wrong, grace covered him. Now that he can see, maybe he's questioning whether it's permissible to walk on this side of the road, cross to the market at this juncture, take this path through to the next town.

The deaf man likely jumped at every noise. The paralytic had to learn how to do everything for himself, and probably still forgot a time or two that he actually could. The woman with chronic bleeding doubtless scouted escape routes in every new situation, just in case she became unclean again and had to get out of there.

These aren't people living healed. These are people stuck in the details, just as so often, we are. That is why we don't hear more about them in the Gospels.

When we're stuck in the details, we lose the story.

The story is that the demons are gone, the blind see, the deaf hear, the mute speak, the lame walk, the unclean are clean, and we are healed.

That is the story. That is His story.

That is the story that, when we get swept up in it, our brokenness does, too. That is the story that takes us to a hillside and a tomb, where a God who could have healed the world in a heartbeat took three long days and we come face-to-face with the Truth about a healing Jesus.

A Jesus who isn't instantaneous like we'd prayed for. A Jesus who never turned away from pain Himself and doesn't turn our pain away.

But who, when we stop praying with one eye open and submit to Him in honest prayer, answers. Fully and completely. He comes and embraces us as we reach out to Him, touches our lives, speaks a word, and wraps us up in the story He's telling.

It's a story in which we see from new eyes, hear from opened ears, hope from a mended heart, jump to our paralyzed feet, pick our mat, and walk into a life lived healed.

# \ Pray for Me /

*Pray for me.*

Three dreaded words that leave us scrambling for something worthy to say on behalf of the individuals in our congregations, in our communities, in our social networks who are requesting our intercession. Friends, family, and complete strangers aching for the Lord to hear them. People for whom we ought to pray, perhaps for whom we even want to pray, but for whom we have no earthly idea exactly how to pray.

The prayer request is nothing new. Throughout Scripture, sinners came to the prophets, apostles came to the churches, and God came to His people, asking them to pray for one another.

Pharaoh asked Moses to pray away the plague. "Pray that the Lord will take the frogs away from me and my people." (Exodus 8:8)

King Jeroboam beseeched the man of God to pray for his healing. "Please make an appeal to the Lord your God, and pray for me so that I can use my arm again." (1 Kings 13:6)

Paul is a man who both makes prayer requests and fulfills them. He does not hesitate to ask for the prayers of the faithful. "At the same time also pray for us. Pray that God will give us an opportunity to speak the word so that we may tell the mystery about Christ. ...Pray that I may make this mystery as clear as possible." (Colossians 4:3-4) And he reminds them that he is praying for them. "We always thank God, the Father of our Lord Jesus Christ, in our prayers for you." (1:3)

James tells us to confess and to pray, for the prayers of a righteous person are powerful and effective. (5:16) Not that we are particularly righteous, but when we are able to receive another's confession and heart with an honest measure and come before our Lord on their behalf, we come close to a righteous offering.

In the book of John, Jesus prays aloud for God's people. Not for everybody, but for a specific people who God has put on His heart. "I pray for them. I'm not praying for the world but for those you gave me, because they are yours." (17:9)

Certainly, then, there is a Biblical mandate that we pray for one another. At least for those that God has given us, because they are His.

Samuel went so far as to say it would be sin not to pray for the people, as they had asked him to do. "It would be unthinkable for me to sin against the Lord by failing to pray for you." (1 Samuel 12:23)

We must go further and believe that not only is it unthinkable for us to ignore our duty of praying for one another, it is unthinkable that we are so content to cover them in superficial prayer.

The persons on our prayer list have come there because they believe in the power of prayer and in the promise of God that He hears us when we pray. And more specifically, that where two or more are gathered, He promises to be there. (Matthew 18:20) The prayer list is a way to gather two or more together before God in possession of the same petition.

Yet we cheapen man's faith and God's promise by working methodically through a bunch of names, saying each one, maybe even out loud, and moving onto the next. Not really knowing what to pray nor how to pray, so settling for not really praying.

We pray vague prayers, at best; platitudes at worst, all in the name of telling someone that we have prayed for them.

"Dear Lord, I just ask right now that you be with Stephanie. And with Bill. And come alongside Jeff. And I pray for Deborah for her broken heart, and for a job for Clint. Amen."

It has a *Dear Lord* and an *amen* and we hit every name on the list, but the only thing we are honestly able to tell our list-ers is that for half-a-second, we thought about them while we almost prayed and said their name when we suspected God might be listening. They graciously thank us and life goes on.

But we can do much better praying for our friends. We can do much better petitioning for our families. We can do much better honoring our communities.

> When we pick our prayer list, we are to take our heart in our hands, too.

We can do so much better before our God.

We have a responsibility to discipline ourselves into praying honestly for our prayer list. We have been called to pray for another with the same integrity with which we pray for ourselves.

When we pick up our prayer list, we are to take our heart in our hands, too, and offer what we honestly have to honor the heart of a friend who is honestly yearning. That is the heart of honest prayer.

It is called compassion.

*pray*

Compassion is the heart by which God responds to His people.

Nehemiah says it was because of compassion that the Lord did not abandon His people in the wilderness. (9:19) He goes on to say of the Lord that, "When [your people] began to suffer, they cried to you. You heard them from heaven. You gave them saviors to rescue them from their enemies because of your endless compassion. ...You rescued them many times because of your compassion." (9:27-28)

The Psalmist confidently declares our Lord as full of compassion. "The Lord is merciful and righteous. Our God is compassionate." (116:5) Not only is God compassionate, but also "the Lord...has compassion for everything that he has made." (145:9)

Isaiah says the Lord longs to be gracious to His people and "He rises to have compassion on you." (30:18) By this compassion, He "will lead them and guide them to springs." (49:10) The Lord's compassion is the means by which He brings us into life.

And let us not forget that Jesus was the master of compassion. When He saw the crowds, He had compassion on them. (Matthew 9:36, 14:14, 15:32) Two blind men called out to Him on the road, and when He heard them shouting, He had compassion. (Matthew 20:34) In the story of the prodigal son, it is the father's compassion that sends him running toward his returning son. "He ran to his son, put his arms around him, and kissed him." (Luke 15:20)

Jeremiah says the Lord's heart yearns for His child, for whom He has great compassion. (31:20)

The Lord's heart yearns where He has great compassion. So it is through compassion that our hearts yearn, as well, for the pains and needs and petitions of our brothers and sisters, those whose names are written on our lists. Those God has given to us.

Compassion is the heart of our prayer for another.

The Lord commands His people to be compassionate. "This is what the Lord of Armies says: Administer real justice, and be compassionate and kind to each other." (Zechariah 7:9)

Paul tells the Colossians to clothe themselves with compassion, "as holy people whom God has chosen and loved." (3:12) And he reminds the Philippians that their capacity for compassion comes from Christ Himself. "So then, as Christians...do you have any sympathy and compassion?" (2:1)

Then it is joy, Paul continues, to have the same attitude and the same love.

The same attitude and the same love enable us to enter a heart of compassion in prayer and connect with those individuals whose names we bring before the Lord. Not in some trite, dutiful way but with appreciation for their situation and a sincere commitment to honoring both our brother and our God.

*pray*

We don't have to understand every circumstance. We are not required to know exactly what it is like to be in our brother's shoes. But we have to stop pretending we haven't got a clue.

When we pray for someone else, we have to be willing to touch that place inside of us that kind of knows what it might be like, that understands what it would feel like if those questions were in our heart.

We pray for those afflicted with cancer or disease. Maybe we have never had that diagnosis, but we have all had moments when our bodies have failed us. Times when we have not been able to do the things we wanted to do. Moments when we questioned whether we would have more time to do things. Times when we ran out of time and then it was too late.

We pray for the unemployed. Maybe we are blessed to have a job. But we know what it's like to long for stability. We know what it's like to worry about tomorrow. Heck, we know what it's like to worry about today.

We pray for those whose families are falling apart, who are facing divorce or separation or distance or dysfunction. Maybe we have been fortunate to keep close contact with those that we love. But we have all lost someone, somewhere. We know what it is to not be able to touch that someone any more, to not be able to share the stories, to not be able to talk around the table. We know the void and the emptiness where someone we once loved used to be, and now there is nothing, and it aches.

> It doesn't matter if we've been "there." We have been "here."

It doesn't matter if we've been "there." We have been "here." Honest prayer isn't about circumstances; it is about the heart. A heart that is able to enter its own depravity is one that is filled with compassion. From such a heart flows honest prayer.

No, maybe we don't know what "this" or "that" is like. But we pray for a heart that is questioning out of our heart that has questioned. We pray for the aching out of our ache. We pray for the lost out of our wandering. We pray for the scared out of our fear. We pray for the worried out of our worry. We pray for our brothers and sisters out of a heart of compassion, knowing we are not so very different.

The prophets knew this. They never considered themselves greater than the people for whom they were interceding before God. They never considered themselves apart from the troubles of the people for whom they prayed. They were a part of it.

When the prophets prayed for the people, they weren't praying for "them." They prayed for "us." They included themselves in the fallen, the sinful. They knew they were part of the people of God and that the people's unrighteousness included them, too.

Habakkuk spoke before the Lord and questioned him. "Didn't you exist before time began, O Lord, my God, my Holy One? We will not die! O Lord, you have appointed the Babylonians to bring judgment. O Rock, you have destined them to correct us." (1:12) He prayed to *his* God, but he did not consider himself separate from God's people. He was one of "us," just as subject to the Babylonian oppression as any other man.

The prayer of the prophet at the end of Lamentations reflects this pray-er's position as a member of the Lord's community. "Remember, O Lord, what has happened to us. Take a look at our disgrace!" (5:1) On behalf of his people, the prophet prays, "O Lord, bring us back to you, and we'll come back. Give us back the life we had long ago, unless you have completely rejected us and are very angry with us." (5:21-22) It wasn't about him; it was about "us."

Daniel, the man of God who stood alone with the hungry lion, prayed to His Lord for the sake of his people. "I prayed to the Lord my God. I confessed and said, 'Lord, you are great and deserve respect as the only

God....We have sinned, done wrong, acted wickedly, rebelled, and turned away from your commandments and the laws. We haven't listened to your servants the prophets, who spoke in your name.... You, Lord, are righteous. But we – the men of Judah, the citizens of Jerusalem, and all the Israelites whom you scattered in countries near and far – are still ashamed because we have been unfaithful to you.'" (9:4-7) No other man of Judah stood beside Daniel in the lions' den, yet Daniel prayed for them all when he prayed for himself.

There is no brokenness, no need, no rebellion, and no faith under God of which we are not a part. So it is not a stretch to pray for one another with an honest heart, knowing we are just as guilty, just as broken, just as aching as the man standing next to us.

Our prayer on behalf of another is not some mere mention of a name. It is our way of standing with them, carrying them to Christ, taking them to the Lord as an army of two or more, where God promises to come alongside us. And taking away the agony of fighting alone.

Paul says, "Brothers and sisters, I encourage you through our Lord Jesus Christ and by the love that the Spirit creates, to join me in my struggle. Pray to God for me...." (Romans 15:30)

It is upon us, then, in the midst of our prayer lists, in our pursuit of an honest prayer, by the power of the Lord Jesus Christ and by the love – that is, compassion – that the Spirit creates, to join one another in our struggles. And pray to God.

\ **Do Not Be Afraid** /

We fold our hands, bow our heads, close our eyes and for God to answer, for Him to come, for Him to be with us or our friends or our families. We pray for God to speak directly into our lives. We pray for Him to act on the same plane we have to live in, this mess of a world that's turning our world into the mess that drove us to our knees in the first place.

Then we're terrified when He actually does it.

Because the God we think we know never just pops in for a visit, even if we invited Him to. If God shows up, there has to be some earth-shattering, about-to-be-shaken reason for Him to be here.

Which is why when He comes, we don't rush to Him with open arms and depths of gratitude; we cower in a corner and wait for Him to speak. To tell us just how much trouble we're in or about to be in.

Then He speaks, and His first words are, "Do not be afraid."

He spoke these words to the priest Zechariah, who was burning incense at the altar when God dropped in for a visit. *Do not be afraid, Zechariah. I have heard your prayer.* (Luke 1:13)

He spoke these words to Mary, who thought she had a moment alone. *Do not be afraid, Mary. I am giving you a child.* (Luke 1:30)

He spoke these words to disciples stuck on a boat, tossed by waves in the midst of a storm. *Do not be afraid, friends. I am coming to you on the water.* (Matthew 14:27)

In all of these encounters, He starts with a command: Do not be afraid.

They were already afraid. God did not sneak in quietly, unassuming. He didn't slowly approach, whispering, "Don't be afraid." He didn't make a casual entrance, knocking on the door and waiting to be let in. One minute, there's nothing. The next minute, there's God. Or a messenger of God. In the flesh. And in that first reflexive gasp of air, while Zechariah, Mary, and the disciples struggled to catch their breath, they were already afraid.

Oh. My. God. …is here….

Thus, "do not be afraid" are prudent first words from a wise God. He didn't mean to scare them, of course, but He knew they would be startled. That's why He starts with "do not be afraid," then continues with, "It's Me." Just Me. Just little ol' God. Nothing to be afraid of.

Take a breath.

You can almost imagine the men and women to whom He appeared playfully smacking His shoulder, saying, "Don't *do* that!"

Because this was a God that these men and women knew, or at least knew about. God's not showing up to someone who hasn't heard at least part of His story. God never came to this man or that woman, held out His hand and said, "Hello. Allow Me to Introduce Myself. I'm God." No. He shows Himself to those who know Him and who, in some way or another, are looking for Him.

And they know this is Him.

*pray*

These men and women could have rightfully expected that one day, God might have something to say to them. They were, after all, His people. They considered Him, after all, their very real God. It's just that when He actually shows up, it's almost entirely unexpected.

Zechariah was an old man, beyond the age of having children. He served as a priest, and we can assume that as an old man, he had served for many years. Priesthood wasn't a second career; it was a life. In all those years, he'd probably had a handful of altar experiences, a few times his lot was cast to burn the incense before the Lord. He'd probably locked himself in the Holy of Holies a dozen times before that day. And we know he prayed; when God appeared to Zechariah, He said, "I have heard your prayer." Zechariah knew God.

> It's just that when He actually shows up, it's almost entirely unexpected.

He just probably never expected to see Him. He couldn't have anticipated that on this particular day at this particular time with this particular incense, God Himself was going to show up with a personal message for this old man. He had no reason to think that this Holy of Holies was going to be any different than the one before it or the one before that.

Mary was a Jewish woman. She would have grown up hearing the stories of God, hearing the prophecies about the Messiah. She would have prayed for the coming of the One Isaiah talked about. She would have offered sacrifices at the temple. She would have attended all of the holy days, festivals, and gatherings. Mary knew God.

She just probably never expected He would choose her. She couldn't have anticipated that a lowly virgin womb from such a retched place as Nazareth – can anything good come from there? – sitting by herself doing nothing in particular on a thoroughly average day would be God's choice for the seed of His Son.

The disciples traveled with Jesus. They watched Him heal. They heard Him pray. They listened to Him teach. They saw Him love. They knew the way He liked to cook His fish and what kind of miracles He could work with a measly loaf of bread. The disciples knew God.

They just probably never expected that against gale-force winds, sheets of rain, bolts of lightning, rumbles of thunder, and the dark of the storm, God would step out onto the raging sea to come to them.

We, too, are people who know God, or at least know about him. We have heard His stories. We have read His book. That's why we pray to Him – we have found Him worthy of our prayers.

We just never expect Him to show up. Then He does, and we are afraid. One moment, there was nothing. Now, God. In that first breath of reflexive air, we are afraid. The fullness of God has arrived and that very well means everything is about to change.

*pray*

Maybe things are about to change. Maybe everything. But that's no reason to fear. God answers because He hears you, He chooses you, and He is coming. He is coming to answer your honest prayer. That's all.

Zechariah was burning incense at the altar. This was an offering embedded in ritual, painstakingly laid out in the law of Moses in order that the priests would honor God by getting it right. The prayers he said in the Holy of Holies would have been highly ritualized with no room for words of his own; such would be considered displeasing to the Lord. And you don't want to displease the Lord with your honest prayer in the middle of His old covenant ritual.

But when God shows up, His word to Zechariah is: "I have heard your prayer." The prayer the Lord goes on to answer is not the ritualistic prayer of the incense. He's not responding to the words Zechariah was likely just uttering before the altar. No. He comes behind closed doors to answer the prayers of this man's heart.

Zechariah wants a child. If you have ever known a family struggling with infertility, you know how fervent and pained and raw their prayers are. God shows up to tell this old man that he's going to have that child, and it won't be just any child. This child will be the voice crying in the wilderness. This child will be the precursor to the Messiah. This child will be the guide for a new generation of seekers, preparing the way for the Lord.

I've heard you, Zechariah, the Lord says. And now that we've got a minute, let Me tell you what I'm going to do. I'm going to give you a child.

Mary, so far as we know, was not actively praying when the Lord appeared to her. But the way she responds after a visit from the messenger Gabriel clues us in that this was an answer to her heart, as well. She'd probably never prayed to mother the Messiah, but maybe she'd prayed to be something more than she was. Maybe she'd prayed for God to fulfill His plan in her generation. Maybe she'd prayed for a glimpse of her own purpose. Maybe her prayers centered around finding something greater. After all, this was Nazareth, and there wasn't a lot of promise there from everything we know about the place. She was searching – and likely praying – to not be bound by her hometown or peasant status.

Then God shows up and tells her He has a plan. I'm giving you a child, Mary, He tells her. I'm going to bring you into My story.

It is her response that tells us this must have been her heart. The magnificat, as we call it, is this beautiful pouring out of her absolute joy that God would choose her. Unless there was a burden on her heart for something of God, this is not a particularly predictable response.

God came to this lowly girl from this despised place, spoke His word into her heart and planted His Son in her womb. What He's given her is trouble. Stigma. A story nobody's going to believe. A tough road ahead. Questions and dilemmas and decisions that at any age, nobody wants to have to deal with. Let alone a young girl. Her husband-to-be is nowhere in sight; she doesn't know if he's going to stay with her or stone her. The townspeople aren't hearing this promise from God. Her family, Joseph's family, nobody knows what's happening here. In social construct, she's just received from God a terrible burden.

(This, by the way, is precisely the God we're afraid of. This is the God we fear shows up. This is the God that when God does show up, we're expecting. This God of life-altering, heavy burdens that we feel unqualified and unprepared for and unwilling to take on.)

Mary, however, praises Him for the gift. Knowing how you would react if God so burdened you, don't you think there had to be more to Mary's story than a random holy cameo in one quiet moment? Don't you think there was something that made her almost ready for this or at least, hoping for a moment so holy?

There had to be honest prayer in there somewhere. There had to be a heart that was hungry for the chance to be in God's story. There had to be a thirst that was deeper than any threat. There was something about this woman that enabled her to hear God's word and respond with gracious, excited, beautiful words of her own - My soul magnifies the Lord; My spirit rejoices in God, my Savior. (Luke 1:46-47)

Then there are the disciples, who were either engaged in the most honest prayer they have ever prayed or were too busy trying to save themselves to pray, lamenting that Jesus wasn't with them. Storm-tossed, they were either crying out from scared hearts or preoccupied with their oars and masts and drawing on all of their fisherman knowledge to try to right their boat.

Jesus comes walking to them on the water, and the storm fades. But He hadn't come to calm the winds that tossed their boat.

He came to calm the storm that wracked their hearts. Their lingering questions about the actual nature of their new friend, Jesus. Their constant need for reassurance that what seems to be happening is really happening. The doubts they wouldn't dare speak in front of one another, and certainly not in front of Him, but still harbor in their hearts almost as a back-up plan. In case this story falls apart and they have to walk back into their old lives and explain themselves.

> The God we think we know never just pops in for a visit; there has to be some earth-shattering, about-to-be-shaken reason for Him to come down here. There is. It's you.

Jesus appears to assure them they aren't walking back into anything; they are walking on water. Everything they thought they knew about the world has changed, and this thing is for real. This is what it is. He is Who He is.

Then He steps into the boat, and there are no more questions. The disciples settle into the calming seas and breathe. Storm or not, this is what this is. And this is Jesus.

*pray*

We pray to a God we hope can hear us. We long for a God who will come to answer us. But it's scary to think He might actually show up.

The God we think we know never just pops in for a visit; there has to be some earth-shattering, about-to-be-shaken reason for Him to come down here.

There is. It's you.

He comes behind closed doors to find you at the altar, buried in ritual. Do not be afraid. He hasn't come to talk about incense; He's come to answer your aching heart.

He comes into nothingness to find you in a moment alone. Do not be afraid. He hasn't come to arbitrarily change your story; He's come to invite you into His.

He comes through the storm to find you burdened and busy, tossed about by the waves. Do not be afraid. He's not an optical illusion; He is coming.

He is coming to show you what this is. This is Jesus.

This is the God you pray to. This is the God to whom you pour out your heart.

This is the God who comes and, in that first instinctive reflex, takes your breath away.

Oh. My. God. ....is here....

Do not be afraid.

# \ Holy Moments /

One of the reasons we fear what God might be doing when He shows up is that we question our ability, or our willingness, to go along with Him. We don't know whether we can, or will, do what He asks of us in response to our prayer.

Just look at what God asks His people to do. Abraham, to sacrifice his son. Esther, to stick her neck out in front of the king. Daniel, to walk into the lion's den. Hosea, to marry a prostitute.

These are not the conversations these men and women intended on having with God. These are not the responses they expected to get. When Abraham starts a dialogue about his faith, he couldn't have expected God to respond by testing him. When Esther asked God what could be done, she didn't expect Him to tell her that she was the answer. Daniel thought God would show up before the lions, not among them. Hosea might have had a quieter, more honorable virgin in mind.

These are the stories that make us tremble a little, not at the excitement of being used by God but in absolute fear of being asked by Him. God so rarely asks us for the easy things.

But we cannot condition our prayer on what God's response might be. We cannot diminish our asking for fear of the answer. We have to pray our hearts, ask our questions.

We can't let the next holy moment diminish what this one might be. What we do next is irrelevant to what we pray now. How we answer His answer is its own encounter. We have this chance to pray, and we have to take it. Whether we are ready to take the next step of faith or not.

*pray*

Not everyone can, or will, take that step. But that doesn't mean they missed their holy moment.

To understand, we need look no further than the stories of Jonah, Moses, and the rich young ruler.

The rich young ruler is perhaps the simplest story to follow. His story is in Matthew 19:16-22.

Here is a man who has nearly everything the world could offer him, yet he finds himself wanting more. He wants the eternal life that so many are talking about, and he's heard the stories of this Teacher, Jesus, who can tell him how to get it. So in the midst of Jesus' travels, this wealthy young man appears and asks:

*I have obeyed all these commandments. What else do I need to do?* (v. 20)

It is an honest question. It is a man asking Christ for the one thing the world has not been able to give him, the one thing his heart is still longing for, the one thing that will give him peace at night. And this Teacher is faithful to answer.

*Sell what you own. Give the money to the poor, and you will have treasure in heaven. Then follow me!* (v. 21)

Then, Matthew tells us, the man walked away. And Jesus did not go after him.

He came to God in honest prayer, asking a question, expecting an answer. God honestly answered the man's honest question. That was a moment. What happened next could not diminish that this man had a real, powerful, honest encounter with God. He had a prayer.

As for the next step of faith, he considered God's answer and decided it was a step he could not take. So he walked away and God let him walk. It doesn't change the holy moment that was – the Lord remembered the man enough to include him in His story; the man likely never forgot those few minutes with the Teacher - it only changes the moments that were to come. We will never know what those would have been.

Other times, God does not let a man off so easy. Such is the story of Jonah.

We don't get a lot of Jonah's back story. We don't know what he did in the days leading up to Jonah 1, when God asks him to go to Nineveh. We get sort of a glimpse, perhaps, from his reaction to that request. He responds in disgust, in arrogance, judging and condemning the people of this town that do not live up to some standard in his own mind.

We can imagine, then, that Jonah prayed like a Pharisee – often and devoutly, with a little hint of pride that he was a better man. And he seems more than willing to carry on a debate with the God who has come to commission him.

And God says:
*Go to Nineveh.*

That was a moment. What Jonah decided to do in response to God's voice could not diminish that this man had a real, powerful, honest encounter with God. He had a prayer.

As for the next step of faith, Nineveh was not tops on the destination list. Jonah did not want to go.

Jonah ran away. As far and as fast as he could. And God went after him.

God pursued Jonah onto a ship, into the sea, and rocked him with a storm. He pursued him into the waters and sheltered him in the belly of a whale. When the Lord had Jonah all alone, Jonah cried out to Him. That was another moment.

And again, Jonah heard:
*Go to Nineveh.*
From the belly of a whale, Nineveh looks like a dandy place to be. Covered in fish guts, reeking of three-day-old dinner, Jonah could no longer assert that he was above the Ninevites. He smelled like the garbage that a few days prior, he'd thought those people to be.

God went after Jonah and convinced him to go. He demonstrated that where He's sending him was not such a bad place after all. And now Jonah's story is in God's story. Through one tattered man, God redeemed a village.

Between the extremes of letting you go and making you go, God has a third answer to your next step of faith, and we see that in the life of Moses. (Exodus 3-4:17)

Moses was a Hebrew baby, raised in the house of Pharaoh. He saw from both sides the exploitation of his people – God's people – and he no doubt carried the agony of helplessness with him. He likely prayed adamantly for God to see this injustice and show Himself, rescuing Israel from its oppression and sparing Moses from the double-life of an "Egyptian" Hebrew.

And God replied:
*Lead My people.*
That was a moment. An honest response to an honest heart that was longing to do what was right for God's people. What Moses decided to do in response

could not diminish that this man had a real, powerful, honest encounter with God. He had a prayer.

As for the next step of faith, Moses hesitated. He had all of these reasons why he was not a good candidate to be the leader of God's people, why he could not just walk in and talk to Pharaoh, about how he had a speech impediment, about how he had a reputation – both with the Egyptians and with the Israelites.

Moses wanted to turn away. But God called to him.

He led Moses by miracles, holding his attention with a burning bush and a snaky staff. Keeping Moses engaged in the dialogue, intrigued by the possibilities, and ever-growing in confidence, God showed Himself to the one man He was going to use to show Himself to the nations.

> We are so afraid He's going to arbitrarily change our story, rock our world for the sake of a good storm, test our faith when we're pretty sure that we have none.

Then God does one better. He gives Moses a helper, someone to stand alongside him while God continues to lead. This answers his hesitations, his arguments, his weaknesses, for where he is weak, his brother is strong. Together, they are able to do what God has asked. And Moses becomes a major player in God's story.

Just before he dies, Moses sees the Promised Land.

Because of him, God's people entered it.

*pray*

We are so hesitant to pray because we don't know our ability to follow-through. We don't know whether we are willing to come when God says to come, whether we will go when He says go, whether we will speak when He says speak. We aren't sure whether we will agree with Him on what is the right place for us or when is the right time or what we are capable of doing, even with Him.

We are so afraid He's going to arbitrarily change our story, rock our world for the sake of a good storm, test our faith when we're pretty sure that we have none.

That's not His style. God isn't about just changing our story; He is inviting us into His, whether we have one single moment like the rich young ruler, an entire village like Jonah, or a life's journey like Moses.

Some of us will walk away, and God will let us go. If from an honest heart, we ask and hear His invitation and still choose to walk away, it does not change one holy moment we had with Him. It only changes all of those that were to come.

Some of us will run away, and God will come after us. If from an honest heart, we hear His invitation and choose to run, it does not change one holy moment we had with Him. It only changes all of those that were to come.

Some of us will turn away, and God will call to us. If we hear His invitation and choose to turn away, it does not change one holy moment we had with Him. If we see Him standing in front of us and choose, even just a little, to trust, it does not change one holy moment we had with Him. If He sees us shaking and sends a brother to stand alongside, it does not change one holy moment we had with Him.

It only changes all of those that are to come.

If we cast aside our questions and concerns, our fears and our angst, our doubts and our dilemmas, and pray for simply the sake of connecting in one moment with our

God, whatever we do next, whatever we decide after we have spoken and heard, does not change one holy moment we had with him.

It only changes all of those that are to come.

Whatever holy moment there is to come, we have at least this one. We have a prayer.

Let us pray.

# \ Holy Words /

We pray, hungry for a holy moment, but some days, it hardly seems He and we are speaking the same language.

God talks about things like mercy and grace and forgiveness, but mercy doesn't make the mortgage payment, grace doesn't give good news, and forgiveness fails to fashion opportunity.

We want to pray about such things, but how?

We are told to "keep your thoughts on whatever is right or deserves praise: things that are true, honorable, fair, pure, acceptable, or commendable." (Philippians 4:8) Whatever is right? Our hearts are burdened with all that is wrong!

He tells us not to worry about things like what we'll eat or what we'll wear (Matthew 6:25), and we broaden that to mean we shouldn't pray about such things, either. That God isn't interested in the nitty-gritty of our lives. That we have to set our minds on higher things and ignore our petty troubles because God doesn't want to hear about it.

Like the God who created Job didn't want to hear about it.

For thirty-seven chapters, Job laments his situation as a man cursed on this earth. For thirty-seven chapters, his friends do their best to console him by spouting sermon points about God. For thirty-seven chapters, Job faces his troubles and cries out to God for healing. And if not healing, at least answers. In chapter 38, God finally speaks.

The words of God are not what a weary Job wants to hear. They are not the answers we hope for when we pray. God's answer seems kind of harsh, and it's easy to think God has little care for Job's temporal troubles.

"Brace yourself like a man!" God tells Job. "I will ask you, and you will teach me." (38:3) Then for four long chapters, God questions Job about creation.

"Are you questioning Me, Job?" God says. "Can you recreate even the tiniest organism in My creation? Do you know about the lioness? The crow? How about the mountain goats, the wild donkey, the wild ox, the ostrich? Have you ever made an ostrich, Job?

"What about the horse? The birds of prey? What exactly is this fault that you find with Me? Have I not created all of this?"

Job interjects, but only briefly. He has nothing more to say to his God. "I'm so insignificant," Job answers. Imagine him stuttering a bit in trembling before the Lord. "How can I answer you? I will put my hand over my mouth. I spoke once, but I can't answer – twice, but not again." (40:3-5)

Sorry, Lord, Job's says. Sorry that I dared to speak. Sorry that I dared to question. Sorry that I dared to say this wasn't enough or this doesn't make sense. I have no right to speak before You, so I'm just going to shut up now.

Sound familiar?

But God doesn't let him off the hook. No, God persists. "Brace yourself like a man! I will ask you, and you will teach me." (40:7) Then God spins into harsher, harder questions. The Bible says God stormed.

"What can you defeat, Job? What evil is there among you that you have strength over? Are you at all like Me? Can you thunder?" God thundered.

"Can you defeat even one beast, even one piddly beast? Behemoth? Leviathan? Anything? No? Then why do you question Me the way you do?"

The scene ends with Job retracting his words, apologizing for his questions, and sitting in the dust and ashes to show his remorse for such foolish lament. (42:6)

*pray*

To avoid the same covered-in-ashes, humble apologies fate as Job, we divide our lives into two categories: the holy and the unholy. The holy, we take to the throne of God. The unholy – our circumstances, our mundane lives, our trivial temporal troubles – we take on our own shoulders, all the while lamenting that no good and gracious God is coming along to help.

He has not come along because we have not asked. We have considered Him to be so far above this world that He can't understand its troubles. We have assumed He cares so little for our problems here that we've stopped pestering Him about them.

We have forgotten that Jesus washed His feet like any other traveler. We have forgotten that He understands the dirt down here.

> We have forgotten that Jesus washed His feet like any other traveler.

He understands hunger, the way food feeds both the body and the soul. He knows that a hungry person is no good for the journey and that a little bit of food goes a long way. That is why we have two stories of Jesus feeding the masses before sending them home.

"I feel sorry for the people," Jesus said in Matthew 15:32. "They have been with me three days now and have nothing to eat. I don't want to send them away hungry, or they may become exhausted on their way home."

They need fuel for the journey, He said. Yet we read the verse, also in Matthew, where God tells us not to worry about what we will eat, and we decide that hunger is not worth praying over.

Then what are we to do with a Lord who feeds the hungry?

He understands money, the way people worry about every little penny. He knows how a farmer pays his laborers, how a government collects taxes, how a tax collector skims a little off the top. One of His disciples was caught in tax trouble, an on-the-spot audit that he did not know how to answer. The answer was this:

"So that we don't create a scandal, go to the sea and throw in a hook. Take the first fish that you catch. Open its mouth, and you will find a coin. Give that coin to [the tax collectors] for you and me." (Matthew 17:27)

He never said that taxes were not His concern. He did not say there were more important things to deal with. He provided the money that Peter needed to pay the tax. Yet we read a verse like Psalm 23:1 that says, "The Lord is my Shepherd. I have everything I need," and we decide that money (or lack thereof) is not worth praying over.

Then what are we to do with a Lord who provides?

He understands family, friends, and social status. He knows the way that sisters fight, the way that brothers bicker, how good friendships can turn sour, and how a person's reputation so often precedes him. He knows about loneliness and shame and life on the outskirts. Which is why we have stories of Jesus meeting every man, every woman, every child just where they were and loving them through their questions.

You keep a nice house, Martha, He said. But that's not Mary's thing. And Mary, you have chosen this, and I'm happy to have you here.

James, He continued, there's no reason to argue. Nobody knows whether you or John or both of you or neither will have a place of honor in the age to come.

Give generously to one another, He advised. Do not hold back a good thing from your neighbor, and do not expect something better in return. Honor one another.

Woman, your faith has healed you.

Quiet! This woman has given Me a great gift.

Then neither do I condemn you.

Please accept a drink of living water.

I am having lunch today with the tax collector. Won't you join us?

These were answers to questions we'd hardly consider holy. They were questions we wouldn't dare ask God. They were the things we talk about with our friends. They are the aches, the laments, the troubles we discuss with our loved ones.

"Nobody appreciates my meatloaf!" Martha griped.

"I'm the better brother," James and John argued.

"I can't live like this any more," said a woman whose doctors could not heal her.

"I don't have anything worthy to offer," she cried as she poured out perfume on His feet.

"This is not my finest moment," admits a nearly-naked woman in front of a crowd armed with stones.

"If I never have to walk to this blasted well again, it will be too soon!" said a ragged woman on the edge of town.

"You know I'm a tax collector, right?"

These questions don't seem right or praiseworthy. These are not honorable, acceptable, or commendable things. These are not the pure things we are supposed to think about, and therefore bring before our God.

Oh, but these moments are absolutely pure.

All of these individuals dared to be as they were before Jesus. They dared to be pure. Martha was a little OCD; Mary a little quieter. Until her brother died, and can't you just imagine her screaming and crying and pounding her fists on Jesus' chest when He shows up a few days too late?

> Oh, but these moments are absolutely pure.

James and John fought the demons of arrogance and pride, arguing over who could be the greatest in the Kingdom.

An unclean woman bled through the crowds for the chance to touch His robe, not thinking she had to be clean enough first but trusting that He would make her clean.

A sinful woman walked uninvited into a dinner party to pour out the gift that she had on the feet of the Jesus she longed to meet. A sinful woman toiled at a well, hiding from the whispers yet baring her soul to a thirsty man who would just happen to be the Messiah. A woman caught in adultery, stood exposed before Jesus by an angry mob.

They came pure, and while things kind of seemed like a mess, it is their authenticity that invited a holy moment. It was their openness that made an honest prayer. And God met every single one of them right where they were.

*pray*

Honest prayer is not about what we bring to God; it is about how we bring it. It is about whether we are coming in an honest heart with something that really matters to us, even if it doesn't seem so holy. It is understanding that while God tells us not to worry about what we will eat or what we will wear, He is still the God who knit clothes for Adam and Eve in the Garden, fed the five thousand, fed the four thousand.

Honest prayer is knowing that if it matters to us, it matters to God. That is the essence of love. We need never worry about having questions about the unholy; we need only concern ourselves with unholy questions – those questions we ask that ignore our honest aching.

God knows this place is not perfect. But He put you here with the promise that He would be right beside you through all of it. The mercy and the mess.

I know. You're still wondering about Job and all of God's seemingly unrelated questions in answer to a man's misery. I don't know. Maybe they were too good of friends. You know the way you have those friends that you tease mercilessly, rib often, and sarcastically joke with because you understand each other that way? That is the impression I get from Job.

Because what I do know is that Job didn't walk away from that encounter defeated. He didn't lose faith or lose heart; he was restored by the interaction He had with God, even though it seems kind of harsh to some of us. It was the answer that worked for Job, and God knew it, so they shared that holy moment.

We can share this one.

Not everything is righteous. Not everything is holy. Not everything is commendable or honorable or acceptable. Not everything is pure. But we can bring a pure offering before Him when we pray with an honest heart and ask Him to meet us where we are. Right here in the dirt.

Then, in the mess, He kneels to wash our weary feet. To answer the troubles of a tired journey, whether they seem holy or something less. Because it matters to Him.

As soon as we tell Him it matters to us.

## \ Why /

What matters most to us is not *what* God is doing or not doing. It is not *when* God is or is not doing what He is or is not doing. What matters most to us is *why*.

*Why* is a question from a burdened heart, a person looking for perspective, a man searching for meaning. Meaning, we think, makes sense of this mess. If only we could know why, if only we knew what this moment means, then we could find the strength or the courage or the faith to carry on.

Which is why we ask *why*. *Why* tells us whether this matters. *Why* tells us what this does. *Why* tells us if this makes a difference. *Why* tells us what we're doing here.

*Why* tells us what Romans 8:28 only hints at:- it tells us what the good is for which God is working all things together.

Some of us need a *why* to convince us. We need to understand the end to justify the means. We need to know what we get out of this situation before we walk into it. We use the answer to *why* to justify whether we will or will not.

Some of us need a *why* to move us. We need to know the destination before we set off on a holy adventure. We need to know where we're going before we move from where we are. We use the answer to *why* to decide whether we will go on this journey or just go home.

Some of us need a *why* to strengthen us. We need to understand the bigger things at play. We need to know the greater good at stake before we bet the house. We use the answer to *why* to either stand up or stay down.

Some of us need a *why* to teach us. We need to understand the way God thinks. We need to know how He views a situation so we can see Him, and our circumstance, with new eyes. We use the answer to either follow or flee.

We decide what we're doing or not doing, who we are or who we aren't, based on our understanding of *why*.

*pray*

*Why* is our biggest question, yet it is not one often seen in the Scriptures.

God blesses Abraham and Sarah with a son, long past the time when she should have been able to have one. A few years into young Isaac's life, God directs Abraham to sacrifice his long-awaited son on the mountain as an offering pleasing to God. Abraham wailed. He cried. He probably tore his clothes in grief.

But he never asked why.

Unhesitatingly, Abraham hiked with his son up the mountain, holding onto all of his questions and doubts and fears as tightly as he held his young son's hand. He had enough faith to climb to the mountain even when he wasn't sure he had enough for the sacrifice at the end of the road. He knew God had sent him to this place for this moment.

> We decide what we're doing or not doing, who we are or are not, based on our understanding of *why*.

Did it matter why?

Would Abraham's story be somehow different if he had dared ask why and God had answered him? Would it have changed things for Abraham to clearly know that

## Why

God was testing his faith? It would have changed things, of course. The climb would have been an exercise in futility, and not a testimony of faith, if Abraham had known what God would do on that mountain.

Abraham had to climb the mountain without knowing why. And there in the bushes was his answer. The answer was faith. His.

God sent Jonah to the original sin city – Nineveh. Jonah, a fairly average guy, refused to believe that was his kind of place. He whined. He complained. He protested. He ran away, then stowed away, trying to get away.

But he never asked why.

After a short cooling off period in the belly of a whale, God sent him again. *Go to Nineveh*. Still, Jonah did not ask why. He did go, though. He understood God was sending him to this place for this moment.

Did it matter why?

Would Jonah's story have changed if he knew what God would do in this little town through this simple man? It would have changed, of course. It would have been an entirely different narrative if Jonah had gone to Nineveh knowing he would save it. A tale of confidence, maybe arrogance, and the greatness of a man.

He had to go to Nineveh not knowing why. And there in the mirror was his answer. The answer was redemption. His.

Jesus called the disciples away from their day jobs. James and John, Andrew and Simon, Matthew and the seven others, heard only simple words. *Come. Follow me.* They dropped their nets, abandoned their families, left their stations and started to walk.

And they never asked why.

They spent three years traveling the region with the famed Teacher, experiencing the highs of His healing ministry and the lows of persecution. They were forsaken by the Pharisees and forgiven by their Rabbi and many other things between.

Did it matter why?

Would we think differently of James and John, Andrew and Simon (Peter), Matthew and the others, if they had asked God why He chose them and He had answered? Would it change things to know what it was about these men that made them worthy to be the twelve? It would have changed things, of course. We would add a worth narrative to the story of God, a distraction from the relationship between as we are and as we are called.

They had to go without knowing why. And there in the Upper Room was their answer. The answer was mission. Theirs.

God commissioned Noah to build a boat. Not just any boat, but a vessel large enough to hold the world. An ark to shelter every living thing from the flood waters of God's fury. Noah had never undertaken such a monumental task.

But he didn't ask why.

He had to build that ship not knowing why. And there in the rainbow was his answer. The answer was the promise. God's.

God set Hosea's heart on a prostitute. A man of God, he could have been honored but God asked him to humble himself, to make himself despised among his people, in favor of the larger story.

And Hosea didn't ask why.

He had to marry a woman of ill-repute without knowing why. And there in the marriage bed lay his answer. The answer was love. God's.

God buried Lazarus in a tomb.

## Why

Standing face-to-face with the God who resurrected him, Lazarus still never asked why.

He had to arise not knowing why. And there, in the tender touch of a teary Teacher, was his answer. The answer was life. Eternal.

*pray*

Our *why* is always half a question. We are either usually asking why *this*? Or why *me*? And sometimes, both – why is *this my* burden?

It's an honest question. It is an aching question in a search for meaning, to make some sense out of all that this is. To make sense of this world. To make sense of ourselves. To make sense of our God.

It makes sense we're always asking *why*.

But don't expect much more than a holy "because I told you so" in reply.

That is all God is going to give you up front.

Why?

Because God wants to show you more than that He is faithful.

Had Abraham known what God would do on that mountain, the moral of the story would have been that God does what He says He will do. Had Jonah foreseen his own redemption in Nineveh, the answer would have been that God is who He says He is. Had the disciples known ahead of time where their mission would lead them, had Noah understood the saving grace of the ark, had Hosea appreciated the analogy of the prostitute, had Lazarus expected to open

> God wants to show you more than that He is faithful.

his eyes, all these men would know about God is that He is faithful.

God does what He says He will do.

Which is a good story, but not a great God. Without knowing why, these men went and did and lived and loved and built and buried and borne again, and in the process, they discovered something more.

He is faithful, yes. We see that. But we also see faith. And redemption. And journey. And promise. And love. And life.

We think we have to know why, but we don't. We only need to know that God brought us to this place for this moment.

Does it matter why?

*Why* is in the discovery. It is in the journey from question to answer, from here to there. It is in the risk it takes to go, do, follow, obey, and believe in the God who sent you.

Were God simply to tell you why, your story (and His) would change. It would have to. An answered why negates its own question. You cannot show faith if you know there is a ram in the bushes. You cannot receive redemption if you have not seen your own rebellion. You cannot choose mission if you see clearly the path. You cannot hold promise if you anticipate the rainbow. You cannot know love if you think it's a fable. You cannot have life if you don't embrace death.

These things are never in the *why*. They are always in the journey. And when you discover these truths, what you find convinces you. It moves you. It strengthens you. And it teaches you.

Ask *why*. Pray *why*. Cry out *why*.

But be ready to discover the answer as God leads you. Uncovering *why* tells you what you're doing or not doing, who you are or who you aren't. It also shows you who God is, and it is on the mountain, in the whale, in the cities, on the boat, in the arms of the prostitute, and in the grave where you find Him more that simply faithful.

You also find that He is good.

You never would have known that if He'd ever told you why.

## \ Strangely Warm /

God may not tell you why, but He is still talking with you. And through prayer, you are talking to Him. But how do you know that He hears you? How do you know that you're hearing Him?

The answer is simple: you get the warm fuzzies.

Stop laughing. This is Biblical.

Near the end of Luke, two disciples are walking along the road to Emmaus. Jesus is in the tomb, or so they think. It's been three days since they last saw Him, and they are still a little lost. And a lot bummed.

So the two men are walking along, talking about everything that's happened. Maybe talking about a hope lost. After all, it's been three days, and they should have seen Him by now. Didn't He promise that much? I imagine them kicking the dirt with their sandals, scuffling their feet along the way.

Then a man runs up to meet them. A fellow traveler, a guy headed in their direction. "What are you talking about?" the man asks, seemingly unaware. And the disciples go into the story, looking at the man incredulously, asking, "How have you not heard?"

The three talk for a little while before preparing to part paths. Before they turn their separate ways, the disciples' eyes are opened and they see that this man, this strange man, is Jesus. They finally recognize Him, just as He is taken away before their very eyes.

On the edge of town, they stood for just a minute. Maybe two or three or ten minutes. They stood there wondering how they could have missed it, talking with each other about the signs they maybe should have seen. This was Jesus, they knew, and yet, they hadn't known it. How had the risen Messiah escaped their sight for so long?

One turns to the other and offers a single observation that even the Messiah couldn't have hidden: "Didn't our hearts feel strangely warm as he talked with us on the road…?" (Luke 24:32)

Didn't we have the warm fuzzies?

These were men who knew what it was like to talk with Jesus. They had lived with, worked with, and traveled with Him for the last three years of His life. They had heard Him preach, heard Him speak, heard Him share tender moments with a sinful woman and a rich man and a widow and a tax collector. They had shared many of those tender moments with Him themselves.

They had both spoken to and listened to the tangible Christ. So they knew for sure what it felt like to be heard by and to hear from God. In those surreal moments around the campfire, frying the day's catch, reliving the day's stories, you can imagine they got the warm fuzzies just sitting there. In the presence of God Himself.

> When God is within reach, you just can't escape the warm fuzzies.

Not long after those moments seem to be over, they're walking down a common road, talking to a common man, and suddenly He becomes Jesus in front of them before disappearing in an instant. They look at each other and conclude, "Duh. Of course that was Him! I was tingling. Were you tingling? Didn't you feel strangely warm?"

When God is within reach, you just can't escape the warm fuzzies.

## Strangely Warm

*pray*

This is not an entirely unfamiliar feeling for us. It's the feeling we get when the story turns out the way it's supposed to – when true love wins, when the lost find their way, when warriors return safe. We flush a little warm when an outpouring of love answers the void of the needy, when unexpected help meets an unanticipated need, when people step up to help one another in times of trouble and community does incredible things. It sends shivers up our spines to be in the presence of something grander than we could ever imagine – under the stars, a concert hall filled with the last lingering note of the symphony, confetti falling on the home team. We feel fuzzy all over when we find ourselves no longer alone in the battle, when a friend kneels at our bedside and nurses us through illness, when family comes along and refuses to turn away.

Yes, we sort of know this feeling from a few of the best moments this world has to offer.

And these are the same experiences that make us tingle in the presence of God. Because these are the things God is all about.

In God, the story turns out the way it's supposed to. "And we know that God causes everything to work together for the good of those who love God..." (Romans 8:28, NLT) In the original creation, God looked at His handiwork and declared that it was good. Now He is making it good again, for us, and that means we're living a story that ends just how it should - the lost are found. The slaves are freed. The warriors triumph. The world is redeemed. Love wins.

In God, an outpouring of love responds to the void. Adam and Eve hid naked in the Garden, not knowing how to hide their shame. God sought them out and with tender care, pulled them from the bushes and knit together a few fig leaves – creation's first garments – for their comfort. "Don't ever worry and say, 'What are we going to eat?' or 'What are we going to drink?' or 'What are we going to wear?' Everyone is concerned about these things, and your Heavenly Father certainly knows you need all of them." (Matthew 6:31-32) God's love answers the hunger, the thirst, the nakedness and the emptiness in our lives. In Him, our shame is covered. Our hollowness, filled.

In God, we are in the presence of something grander than we could ever imagine. "Look at the sky and see. Who created these things? Who brings out the stars one by one? He calls them all by name. Because of the greatness of his might and the strength of his power, not one of them is missing.... Don't you know? Haven't you heard? The eternal God, the Lord, the Creator of the ends of the earth, doesn't grow tired or become weary. His understanding is beyond reach." (Isaiah 40:26, 28) The God to whom we pray created the stars one by one. He cast them into the heavens, and He sustains them there. Though we cannot fathom it, His tender understanding of Creation wraps around us, enveloping us in His grand design, and holding us in the same hand that holds the stars. He does not grow weary of holding us.

In God, we are never standing alone. Gideon was in a winepress, hiding from the invading armies, when God met Him in that secluded place. Zaccheus waited for Jesus in a tree, not able to find a place in the crowds. Jesus saw him immediately. A sister faced the death of her brother with heavy grief, only to find comfort when Jesus arrived. Jesus stands beside you. He stands with you. He's not going anywhere. "And remember that I am always with you…" (Matthew 28:20)

Is it any wonder that we get the warm fuzzies when God is near?

*pray*

The danger if we don't, of course, is neither unfamiliar to us. We have watched movies, envisioning how the story must end, and then something totally different happens. We can picture that, too, but it isn't as satisfying.

Instead of the warm fuzzies, these somethings-less are bittersweet. They have their good moments, their good characteristics, even their good characters and they are oh so close to being *that* moment yet fall tragically short in a way that is nearly forgettable. We walk away, not tingling, but quietly concluding, "Well, that was nice."

This is far too often the same sentiment we have about prayer. We settle for bittersweet. We walk away from our moment with God saying, "Well, that was nice." We resign ourselves to something oh so close to being that perfect story but that falls so tragically short of all that God intended it to be that it's almost forgettable.

> You can't walk away from a real encounter with a real God, an honest answer to honest prayer, with the simple thought that that was "nice."

Prayer should never be forgettable. It shouldn't leave a bittersweet taste in your mouth. You can't walk away from a real encounter with a real God, an honest answer to honest prayer, with the simple thought that that was "nice."

You walk away from an honest answer to honest prayer (if you can walk away at all) with the warm fuzzies. Flushed warm, tingling all over, a little shiver up your spine. You can't help it.

That is what the presence of God does.

That's why honest prayer is more than a good feeling. It's more than a sense of peace. It's even more than a strong confidence. Your prayer encounter is strangely warm or God is a stranger.

That's not to put any pressure on you, the pray-er. Most of us have only prayed a handful of those prayers in our lives, if that many. And Lord knows we don't need any more pressure about getting prayer "right."

This is not about praying right. It is about praying present. If you don't get the warm fuzzies when you pray, the answer is not to pray "better." The answer is to figure out what has come between you and God, what it is that is keeping you from being fully in His presence.

> Your prayer encounter is strangely warm or God is a stranger.

Realizing that you're not all warm and fuzzy should inspire you to bolder prayer. It should stir something unsettled inside you to push through the crud and the circumstance, the ritual and the distance, and step confidently into the presence of God and refuse to settle for anything less.

It should make you pray hungrier, a more raw prayer, pray more passionately out of a burning hunger for your God. It should drive you to your knees, throwing yourself at the feet of the God you're longing to be heard by…and to hear from. If you're not tingling, it is because you are not fully in the presence of God. It ought to make you righteously angry to find out that anything is keeping you from being right there with Him. That something is keeping you from the presence of God.

You ought to be angry, and you ought to throw your heart wide open and throw obstacle out the window and throw yourself at the feet of your God with all of the hunger and ache and longing you can muster.

That's honest prayer. That's yearning. That is being so hungry for God, so thirsty for Living Water, that you will do whatever it takes to enter His presence. And admit it: the very thought is making you tingle right now. That's the presence of the God who hears you, in this moment, listening to honest prayer well up inside your heart.

*pray*

Honest prayer begins in emptiness. It begins in hunger. It begins in thirst for the tangible presence of God. It begins with our letting down our pretenses and embracing vulnerability to fall to our knees in search of the God we're desperate to hear from.

Hearing Him speak does not set your yearning aside; it transforms it. God morphs your yearning into burning. Your whole body becomes engaged in the hearing, in the power of prayer. You're wrapped up in the warmth of His presence, the confident assurance of His hope.

If you don't feel strangely warm when you pray, then you're just talking to yourself. If you're talking to yourself, you might be crazy. That's not prayer.

If you're talking to God, you feel strangely warm. That's prayer.

What? You mean like, every time I pray, I'm supposed to get the warm fuzzies. Every time?

Yes. Every time. And why wouldn't you? What prayer would you pray that you wouldn't want to draw you into His presence? What words would you say that you wouldn't want God to hear? What would you pray that you wouldn't want Him to answer?

Every time you pray, you should come so fully into the presence of God that you can't help but feel strangely warm. And you can't help but feel strangely warm when you are in His presence at all.

It's the one thing God can't seem to hide from His people. Even when you don't really know what God is up to, even when you're not sure if that is Him, even when you're not convinced that He is around, you know God is near by that strangely warm feeling you get with just a whisper of Him.

It's the feeling the disciples had on Emmaus Road. They felt it even when they didn't know it was Him. This strange man who joined them for a few steps of their journey, who discussed these prophetic events and the prophecies themselves with them, who spoke with an odd kind of knowing, made them feel strangely warm.

The same kind of warm they'd felt around the campfire, on the boat, on the hillsides, at Calvary.

The same warmth they'd felt every time they had been in the presence of God.

The same warmth that washes over us when we come fully into the presence of God. The tingle of talking with Him and hearing Him speak.

Come into the presence of God. Bring your full heart and pray.

Don't you feel strangely warm?

## \ In the Name of Jesus /

They are the next-to-last words of almost all of our prayer: "In the name of Jesus." If you're feeling really fancy, you might add a few more adjectives: "In the holy name of Your Son Jesus Christ." If you're feeling exceptionally holy, maybe a bit more: "In the blessed holy name of Your one and only Son, our Lord Jesus Christ."

In the name of Jesus Christ, I pray.

We took this idea from the words of Christ Himself, citing the verse where He taught His disciples and followers to pray in His name. "I will do anything you ask the Father in my name so that the Father will be given glory because of the Son. If you ask me to do something, I will do it." (John 14:13-14)

Thus we tack these few key words onto the end of our prayer, saying that we pray in the name of Jesus, not fully understanding what such a thing even means, so that whatever we've asked will be done. Some even argue that unless you include these few key words, God does not hear you and will not answer and the power of Jesus cannot come. Simply because you failed to mention you were praying in His name.

It is the trap of ritual prayer at its best. These are words to make you worry, words to make you think about getting it right. Did you say *in the name of Jesus*? Are you sure? Then have you even prayed at all?

That is not what Jesus intended. He never said to pray using His name, like a man trying to get a better booth at a restaurant by mentioning he knows the owner. Jesus says to pray *in* His name.

There is a difference.

The Greek used in this passage is not a command to include the name of Jesus in your prayer; it is an instruction to honor the name of Jesus in the way you pray. That is, by honoring His character and mission rather than just invoking His name.

When you pray in the name of Jesus, you pray as a representative of Christ. That means when you're standing at the gate to knock, you are holding a decree signed by Christ Himself. It means you speak in His language and in a posture and a presence that is worthy of bearing His name.

Think about the parable of the wedding feast in Matthew 22, where the invited guests failed to show and the king sent his servants into the streets to gather riff-raff to fill the table. If the king's servants had walked up to people declaring, "Yo! Party at the king's house!" no one would have taken them seriously. It doesn't sound like the king's language.

Nor would they have paid much attention if the servants had arrived with trumpets blaring, unfurling a scroll in the middle of the street and in their best official voices, declaring, "Hear ye, hear ye. The royal most high king doth request your presence at the royal wedding feast to commence immediately in the palace of His Royal Majesty." It sounds like the king's language, but the presence is off.

God's language is somewhere in the middle, bearing full authority in the place where real people live and love.

This is demonstrated by Christ Himself, in the way He interacted and communicated with the persons around Him during three years of ministry.

To the Pharisees who spoke in questions, Jesus spoke in riddles. To the bleeding woman squeezing through the crowds, too scared to even speak His name, Jesus turns and quietly says, "Daughter, your faith has made you well."

To a man harsh with the woman who interrupted his dinner party, Jesus speaks harshly, criticizing his lack of hospitality. And to the sinful woman kneeling at His feet, He speaks tenderly, stroking her fragile heart as she wipes His feet with her hair.

> Jesus was able to meet every heart with His words because He tailored His words to every heart.

To Peter, with all of his doubts, Jesus speaks with affirmation. To James and John, with their egos, He speaks with humbling truth. To Mary Magdalene, with the weight of grief, a risen Jesus speaks with comfort.

Jesus was able to meet every heart with His words because He tailored His words to every heart. He refused to be mired in holy language or diminished into the overly informal. He spoke simply as He was, the fullness of God bringing the full glory of God to other simple men as simply a man. He matched His presence with His words.

Prayer is your opportunity to speak your heart in the name of Jesus. That means you come in the authority of the Christ who sent you and use your King's language. It also means you meet yourself in the place where you live and love and invite Christ to love you there, too.

*pray*

When you come in the name of Jesus, it means you pray as Jesus prayed.

We have a few examples in the Gospels of the way Jesus prayed. We know He prayed in the Garden, just before His betrayal. Mark 14 says He fell with His face to the ground and prayed for God to take the coming suffering away from Him. Three times, He prayed and each time, He concluded, "Not my will, but Yours be done." It was a prayer of submission, both in posture and in prose – fallen on the ground, face bowed, surrendered, surrendering.

Luke tells us that as His ministry grew, Jesus was pressed by large crowds. "But he would go away to places where he could be alone for prayer." (5:16) Mark tells a similar story. "In the morning, long before sunrise, Jesus went to a place where he could be alone to pray." (1:35)

When Jesus prayed, He wanted the moment to be His and God's. He wanted to take His heart without pretense, so He put Himself in a position to do just that. He separated Himself and created space for both prayer and peace, a moment alone with just His God in order to lay His heart wide open. It was a prayer of relationship, in a position to be unencumbered by the daily life.

John 17 is a full chapter of Christ's prayer as He prays over Himself, His disciples, and His church. In this case, He is sitting with His disciples, having a conversation about parables, about meaning, about things they've done and things to come. In the middle of their dialogue, Jesus turns His eyes toward Heaven and begins to pray. It was a prayer of pause, a chance to break out of the busyness of daily ministry and refocus everyone on the God who had put them there.

In Luke 10, Jesus is "filled with joy." His immediate words are, "I praise you, Father, Lord of heaven and earth." (v. 21) It was a prayer of gratitude, a moment of praise.

And before breaking the bread to feed the four thousand and the bread to feed the five thousand, Jesus took the little lunch in his hands, looked up to heaven, and prayed over the bread. It was a prayer of thanksgiving, in recognition of the provision of God for His people.

In the name of Jesus, you position yourself to pray, a prayer of praise or provision or pause, and you pray in a posture that matches your prose.

*pray*

In the name of Jesus, you pray in the presence of Christ. You embrace the God who stands before you and beg for the whole of everything He's got, empowered by His being there.

Think of the men and women who lined the streets as Jesus traveled. Think of the way they called out His name as He walked by. Son of David! Teacher! Rabbi! Jesus! They saw the Lord standing in front of them and understood, in one split second, the absolute power of the Son of God. When their shouts turned His ear, they did not hold back.

Nobody who ever called on the name of Jesus prayed an easy prayer. Nobody asked for the small things. No one held themselves back. They laid their hearts wide open and asked for the hard things, the tough things, the big things that only God could do for them. They asked boldly and expected these things to happen.

No blind man ever cried out, "Son of David! Have mercy on me!" and then hemmed and hawed when he got the Teacher's attention. Well, you see, Jesus, I would kind of sort of maybe like to see again...but if You have something different in mind, then I might be interested in hearing You out. I mean, whatever You want.

No! The blind men cried out, "Have mercy on me!" and when Jesus turned to them, they continued, "I want to see!"

The synagogue leader came and fell on his knees in front of Jesus. That certainly got Christ's attention! And in the next moment, he pleaded, "My daughter has died. If only you would touch her, she would live!" This man knelt in prayer and begged for the impossible.

A Canaanite woman cries out to Him. Lord, Son of David! And the Lord did not answer right away. She kept calling out, Lord! Lord! Finally, Jesus turns to her and says she is not the one He was sent to answer. She was a Canaanite woman, a foreign nation, a despised people. Who had time, or compassion, or mercy for a Canaanite?

Many of us might have looked at Jesus and said, "Oh. Ok. I guess I'll go away, then." But not the Canaanite woman. At that moment, she had everything she needed – the Lord Himself was speaking to her, even if it looked like He was shooing her away. She was not about to give up her prayer when He was so close. So she continues, humbling herself before Him, even calling herself a dog, begging for her daughter's healing.

These men and women saw the living God standing before them, and they couldn't waste the moment. They prayed with hearts wide open, begging for the fullness of all He had while He was close enough that they could touch Him. And that He could touch them.

When we pray, we cannot waste this moment. The fullness of God stands within our reach. In His name, we pray in His presence.

*pray*

## In the Name of Jesus

For most of us, the name of Jesus is just part of the ritual, a few words we tack onto the end of our prayer to ensure that we are heard, to guarantee that we are answered.

But the name of Jesus is power.

It is the power that comes from praying in the language of Jesus, with the grace to meet your heart right where it's at.

It is the power that comes from praying in the example of Jesus, positioning yourself for a relational prayer, offering praise and pause, in a posture that honors your prose.

It is the power that comes from praying in the presence of Jesus, asking for the hard things and pursuing the God who stands before you.

It is the power that comes from knowing that praying in the name of Jesus Christ is more than just signing His name to the bottom of your prayer like some seal of approval or authorization of an answer. It is the power that comes from knowing that praying in the name of Christ is praying in the character of Christ, by whose life we come to know the Father who sent Him. By whose ministry we come to know the God who comes to us. By whose grace we come to know the God who hears us. By whose mercy we come to know the God who answers.

It is the power of Christ.

In whose name we pray.

## \ Amen /

When we've prayed in honest prayer in the power and promise and presence of God in the name of Jesus and poured our aching hearts empty before Him, it is difficult to know what to do in our emptiness. There is a part of us that wants to linger, staying in His presence just a little while longer. There is a part of us that was ready to leave a long time ago. There's a part that feels guilty simply going back to life as we know it. Somewhere in the middle, a heart trying to balance it all.

What we've settled on in this moment is simply an *amen*. One small word that we think says, "Thank You for listening," while indicating that, at least for now, we have said all we wanted to say. It is a word of finality. We have finished praying.

If our *Dear Lord* is the salutation, then our *amen* is the closing. You can almost hear the echo, "Sincerely, Me."

But *amen* is no complimentary closing.

Amen is a Hebrew word meaning "so be it." It is not a goodbye. It is not a "thank You for listening." It is not a "see you next time." At the end of our prayer, the word we leave echoing in our hearts and God's is "So be it."

Everything I just said, God? Yeah. Do that. Everything I just asked You for? You'd better. Everything I just set my heart on? I'm waiting. So be it.

It is kind of awkward, at best, don't you think?

It's not that *amen* is not a godly word or even a Biblical word; it is. But we do not use it in the same context. We have twisted it so much that our use of *amen* today is barely (I'm being kind) appropriate.

The word in Scripture is used to confirm the promise of God.

When a promise, or a promised curse, of God is read aloud to His people in Deuteronomy, their response is "Amen." So be it. So be the things that God has promised, the terms of His covenant, the conditions He has placed on the curse.

Jeremiah uses the word twice – once after God's promise to Him and a second time after someone else testifies to the promise of God.

Nehemiah also uses the word twice, both times as the community's response to hearing about God's covenant and His character.

Paul uses the word repeatedly, each time after he has reminded the churches of God's promise.

In the greatest promise of all, John writes the word in Revelation about the return of the King. "The one who is testifying to these things says, 'Yes! I'm coming soon!' Amen! Come, Lord Jesus!" (22:20) So be it, John the Revelator declares. So come soon!

That's where we see *amen* - a prophet, a judge, a king, an apostle presents the promise of God, and the people proclaim *so be it*. God says this....and the people say, *so be it*. God promises that....and the people say *so be it*. The people use their *amen* to consent to the promise. Whatever God said, let it be so.

We also see *amen* in the Bible as an affirmation of who God is. Someone offers praise and the congregation says *amen*. Yes! That is true! God is good! Hallelujah! I agree.

This was the case in the second use of the word in Nehemiah. (8:6)

Several New Testament writers also use *amen* in this way.

## Amen

"Everything is from him and by him and for him. Glory belongs to him forever! Amen." (Romans 11:36)

"Before time began, now, and for eternity glory, majesty, power, and authority belong to the only God, our Savior, through Jesus Christ our Lord. Amen." (Jude 1:25)

And a*men* in the Psalms is the psalmist's response to the praise of the Lord. The Psalmist praises the Lord, then echoes, "Amen!" So be it. So be praise to the Lord.

This is how we see the word in Scripture. *Amen* is either an agreement to the terms of God's promise or an affirmation of the praise of the Lord. That's it.

> *Amen* is either an agreement to the terms of God's promise or an affirmation of the praise of the Lord.

The closest we come to seeing *amen* in prayer is when Jesus teaches the Lord's Prayer in the Sermon on the Mount, but given that this example is not followed in the rest of Scripture, not even by the apostles or the New Testament writers, we have to question whether He was saying *amen* as a part of the prayer…or saying *amen* to conclude His lesson on the way you should pray. Was Jesus saying, "Dear Lord…Amen"? Or was He saying, "Pray this way….so be your prayers."?

The entirety of God's story suggests the latter.

*pray*

The overwhelming example of *amen* as shown in Scripture is not that of a closing signature. This is a word of affirmation and agreement. This is a word spoken in recognition of God's promise and character. It is a communal commitment to what God has spoken.

Contrast that with the way so many of us pray, and it's clear *amen* is not a great way to end our prayer. We pray, and it is mostly about us. It is about our question, our circumstance, our convenience and then we end by saying, "Yes! I agree with my prayer! Let me have everything I just asked for! So be it."

Or maybe we heard ourselves pray and feel righteous about the whole thing, smile a little to ourselves and declare *amen*. "I am so right!," we exclaim. "My prayer is so right and righteous. Awesome!"

> His Word is the Word. His Word is the way and the truth and the life. My word? Yours? They are much, much less.

It is arrogant, to say the least. The deepest part of us that longs to pray a good and right ritual prayer is offended by this truth, but it's true. At the end of our prayer, when we say *amen*, we are using a word that says, "let it be. Let everything that was just spoken be as it was said." But we have been the ones doing the speaking. We are saying *amen* to our own words, asserting that our word is the word.

So be it, we say. So let our word be the word.

His Word is the Word. His Word is the way and the truth and the life. My word? Yours? They are much, much less.

You can see why *amen* may not be appropriate.

*pray*

Two uses of *amen* throughout Scripture, neither demonstrated as the end of a man's prayer. Then what are we to do with this word that has invaded our vocabulary and rooted itself in our ritual?

# Amen

*Amen* is part of our vernacular. *Amen* is standard. It's fairly agreed-upon. And it is a beautiful word.

It's not that we can't, or shouldn't, pray *amen*. Rather, we should discipline ourselves to pray honoring the word. We have to pray to a good *amen*.

We do this by going back to the word's roots, by praying in the promise, a prayer confirming the covenant of God. That means, in part, we don't ask things of Him that He hasn't promised to give us. It's easy to pray for the things that look like answers – a steady job, a stable family, a secure home – but these don't deserve an *amen*. These things are not your promise. Pray from your heart the deeper questions – questions about worth, about love, about security - and there is a good *amen*.

Praying toward *amen* also means we don't neglect our role in the covenant. Every promise of God is contingent upon the heart of man to honor the gift. We can't pray expecting God to answer everything when we are offering nothing; we have to be willing to live up to our end of the bargain. It's easy to pray for the things that God can give us, but there's no *amen* in that. We have an obligation, too. Pray knowing the promise is us and God together, and there is a good *amen*.

We have to pray in affirmation of the curse. Yes, you read that right. We pray in affirmation of the curses of God because they are just as much the truth of our relationship as His promises. It's easy to remember in prayer the good things of God, but that is only half an *amen*. Pray knowing the consequences of the fallen man and the graciousness of God. There is a good *amen*.

An *amen* prayer prays in the character of God, not asking Him to change but asking Him to change us. Praying true to who He is and who He has promised to be and recognizing that whatever we bring before Him falls short if it is not prayed in the language of His promise. Prayer in the promise takes us to a good *amen*.

An *amen* prayer also praises God, celebrating His nature and His nurture, rejoicing in the way that He is who He says He is. Not in the fact that He is, but in the way that He is – in God the God who is I Am. It is a chance to pray thank you, Lord, and hallelujah. You are awesome. You are everything You said You would be. You are everything. *Amen*.

And an *amen* prayer is an invitation. It is an invitation to the community around us, as in Paul's day, to echo an *amen*.

"Otherwise, if you praise God only with your spirit, how can outsiders say 'Amen!' to your prayer of thanksgiving? They don't know what you're saying. Your prayer of thanksgiving may be very good, but it doesn't help other people grow." (1 Corinthians 14:16-17)

Paul says when you give thanks, when you praise God, someone else ought to be able to say *amen*. You ought to be praising His character, asserting His promises, and exhorting truth that someone else can agree to. Otherwise, what good are you? To say it in another Biblical way, you are a clanging gong or a resounding cymbal if you speak of the Lord and no one else can say *amen*.

That is the true test of a good *amen*. Are you praying in a way that if someone else heard you, they would say *amen*? If not, then maybe you should hold back, as well. A prayer that isn't your best *amen* also isn't your best prayer.

*pray*

Your best prayer is a prayer in the promise and the praise of God.

## Amen

Your best *amen* isn't the end of the conversation; it is another beautiful gift you give to God.

When you pray in the promise and character of God, you give Him your *amen*. You give Him the word at the end of all words that says, "So be it." So be You, God. So be Your promises. So be everything *You* said and everything *You* are and nothing more and nothing less.

So be God, God.

If that's not what your *amen* means, then it's not your best *amen*. If it's not your best *amen*, then you haven't prayed your best prayer. If you haven't prayed your best prayer, maybe you're too deep in the ritual and too far from the relationship.

That is what this journey, this book, has been about. It's been about praying to your best *amen*.

It's hard to know how to walk away from a time of prayer. There's always a part of us that wants to stay longer, a part that wanted to leave a long time ago, and somewhere in the middle, a heart trying to balance it all. Maybe you're tempted to settle for something simple like, "Ok, thanks…" Maybe you prefer a trailing-off, quieting, "uhm…yeah." Or maybe you're fine saying nothing at all and simply walking away.

Maybe you're content with a formal closing, a simple *amen*.

But *amen* is no simple word. It is perhaps the most powerful word we pray, the one final word that gives our whole prayer back to God, who is waiting on the chance to let it be. He is waiting on us to let Him be.

So be it.

## \ Afterword: A New Way Home /

One of the most critical moments of any prayer is the time just after the *amen*. It is the moment when you have prayed and God has heard you; He has answered, and you have heard Him. In those next few minutes, maybe hours, maybe days, you have to figure out how to take this holy moment home.

You have to carry God's answer to the place where you actually live in the everyday you actually push through in the crush of your actual life that is likely the very circumstance that brought you to prayer in the first place.

God has a bit of wisdom for this critical moment: find a detour. Find a new way to go, a new scene to take in, a new path to walk.

Take a new road.

*pray*

God always sends His people a new way.

He tells the man in Mark 8, after restoring his sight, "Don't go back into the village on your way home." (8:26, NLT) As we saw in the chapter on demanding fullness, this man had not come alone to the place where Jesus was teaching. His friends basically dragged him there. They would be waiting on their friend to return; they would want to know everything. The man may want to tell them. But God tells him not to go that way.

To the man healed of leprosy, He ordered, "Show yourself to the priest. Then offer the sacrifice as Moses commanded..." (Luke 5:14) He was sending this man to the temple, probably both the first and the last place the man wanted to go. He wouldn't have been allowed in the temple for as long as he'd had a skin disease and still under the old law, he likely longed to offer sacrifices. Particularly now, an offering of thanks for his healing. But at the temple was the priest, who would have been the one declaring this man unclean again and again. He had probably had routine visits with the priest, always hoping, always praying, to be found clean and never receiving such mercy. The temple, the man longed for; the priest, not so much. But it is where God told him to go.

A woman nearly stoned to death looks up to find Jesus standing there without one ounce of condemnation for her, and His final words are "Go! From now on, don't sin." (John 8:11) She had been caught in the act of adultery, which we can assume was not a one-time thing. Adultery rarely is. She lived from lie to lie, from secret rendezvous to secret rendezvous. This affair likely defined her everyday. This was not just a lifestyle; this was her life. But God tells her not to go back to it.

A new way home has been the design of God's temple from its earliest days. The Lord came to Ezekiel in a vision showed the prophet a floor plan that mandated a new way of leaving. "Those entering through the north gate to worship must leave through the south gate. Those entering through the south gate must leave through the north gate. They must not leave through the same gate they entered. They must leave through the opposite gate." (46:9)

However you came into God's presence, you can't simply go back.

The new way for the blind man, who now could see, was to go it alone. He had depended on others for so

## Afterword

long, to lead him and guide him and go with him, that maybe he had forgotten what it was like to make his own way. Jesus told him to take a new path because he didn't want the man to stay crippled despite his opened eyes. He wanted the man to learn to walk on his own.

The new way for the leper was to meet the priest at the temple. The man had been an outcast for so long; it might have been hard for him to assimilate back into the community, no matter how much he longed to do just that. Jesus sent him to the temple not only to fulfill the old law and be found clean but because the temple was the hotbed of community. Everyone would be there. He wanted the man to find a place. He wanted the man who had for so long been apart from everything to learn to be a part of something.

The new way for the woman was a sinless one. She had spent her life learning how to avoid detection, how to sneak around while sleeping around. She knew the ins and outs of not being noticed. Adultery is an affair of the heart; she was longing for intimacy, for someone to know her and love her. Jesus tells her to sin no more so that instead of knowing how to hide, those around her could know her with nothing to hide. He wanted the woman to learn to be known.

Every time God told His people to take a new way, there was a reason. Somewhere on that road, they encountered an added measure of mercy. It was the answer to their hearts.

*pray*

We are a people who pray and would be content for God simply to answer us, to change our circumstances, to heal, to cleanse, to forgive. We convince ourselves that these are our problems. These things hold us down. If just one thing in our lives could be different, then our everything would change.

That last part is true, but the one thing that must be different is our heart. The one thing that must be different is our truth.

It's one thing for God to come and do what you think you want Him to do – to restore your sight, to cleanse your body, to forgive your sins. But it leaves the nagging question of the heart that isn't changed by circumstance; it is a question only touched by Love.

That is why, although we'd be content for God simply to answer us, God won't settle for so little. He wants a relationship, an extended conversation that doesn't begin when we ask for something and end when we receive it. He wants to go deeper and demonstrate that He's more than just the God who answers us.

He is the God who knows us.

He knows that you want to see again, that you are burdened by the darkness that hides your eyes. But He knows, too, that part of your question is your dependence. You want to stand on your own two feet. You don't want to have to rely on friends or family or neighbors for help. You want to do something for yourself.

Ok, He says. Then find your way home.

He knows that you want to be clean, that you have too long suffered under the burden of being outcast. But He knows, too, that part of your question is your place. You aren't sure where you fit in any more, if anywhere at all. You want to touch the world again and be touched by it.

Ok, He says. Then put yourself in the midst of it all. Go to the temple.

## Afterword

He knows that you'd rather not be condemned today, that you already condemn yourself everyday. But He knows, too, that part of your question is identity. You want someone to know you. You want someone to love you. You want someone to see in you what you wish you could see in you, what you pray to one day see in you.

Ok, He says. Then stop slinking around; sin no more.

God knows what your prayer is asking. But He knows, too, the heart behind that prayer. He's never content to leave you with half an answer; He wants to answer your heart. He does this on the new road.

*pray*

Notice that it's never that God is sending you to a new home, only a new way. He never says you can't go back. He understands you have a life here. He understands you have a job, a family, friends, a routine. He knows you have a home, and He's made you wholly for that place.

But He makes you take a new road to make you holy for that place. So that when you circle back around and run into life as you knew it, you know something more – truth – and while home is nothing new, you feel new in it.

You have a new hope, a courage to believe that things can be different. You have a new faith, a confidence to know that they already are. You have a new God, or at least a new relationship with Him, a Creator who knew you well enough to speak to more than your ears; He answered your heart.

You have been made new. Even though this looks like the same old place, you will never be the same old you.

How could you be?

Change is hard. Different is difficult. We are a people who pray, who hear God's answer, who embrace God's healing, and dare to imagine what life would be like if this all were actually true. We dream what life might look like if our eyes were open to see it. We dream about what we'd do if we felt worthy enough or pure enough or clean enough. If we felt loved enough. We can almost grasp what this holy moment might mean if we could take it with us, back to the grind, to the place where the rubber meets the road. We ache to take this holy moment home.

At the same time, most of us admit that we just don't know how to get there from here. We don't know how to live changed in a life that's not all that different. We don't know how to live different in a day-to-day that hasn't changed.

The answer is in the new road. It is in that place where we accept that more than our circumstances have changed. It is on that journey where we discover that we aren't merely new men; we have a new heart.

A new heart is both humbled and hungered by its prayerful encounter with the God who has heard it. A new heart is thrilled and thirsty after knowing it's been answered. It is precisely this paradox, this ambivalence, this being torn between two things, that allows us to embrace the change that has taken place in us.

Because we are both honoring God for what He has done and holding onto His promise to keep doing it. We are rejoicing over God's incredible power and grace and mercy while inviting Him to bring more of it into our lives. We are living renewed while we're praying for renewal. A new heart grasps what was, what is, and what can be all at the same time.

We don't want to walk away unchanged. We don't want to go back like God was some sort of detour, a day

## Afterword

trip we took to see a Man who happened to be speaking in a town nearby. That's not what we're praying for.

We're praying for more.

And more is precisely what happens when we take a new road home. It's where we find the answers to the questions we're really asking. It's where we learn to stand on our own. It's where we learn to live in community. It's where we learn to let our guard down.

It's where we learn how well God knows us and how deeply He loves us.

A prayerful encounter with God necessarily changes you. You can't go back to the way things were; you can't walk a path you thought you once knew.

How could you?

When you come into His presence from the north, He says head south. From the south, head north. From wherever you've come, go the other way and He will tell you how to get there from here.

*This is what the Lord, your Defender, the Holy One of Israel says: I am the Lord your God. I teach you what is best for you. I lead you where you should go.* (Isaiah 48:17)

Unfold your hands, and take hold of His. He will lead you. He will guide you. He will show you which path to take.

Go to the temple. Go and sin no more. Go a new way. Take a new road.

And God will meet you there.

## NOTES:

Superstition
1. "Superstition." Def. *The Merriam-Webster Concise School and Office Dictionary.* 1994.

Pray Continually
1. "Adialeiptos." Def. *HELPS Word-studies.* Helpsbible.com. 2011

Paradoxology
1. Ken, Thomas. "Doxology." 1674.

## About the Author

Aidan Rogers is a young author from Franklin, Indiana, where she is an active member of Turning Point Church. Since coming to Christ as a teen, Aidan has served on five mission teams, drama ministry, women's ministry, and creative ministry. She also routinely shares devotional thoughts with her congregation.

*Unfolded Hands* is Aidan's second book. Her first, *Recess with Jesus*, continues to do well and is being used as small group material in churches across the nation. She is already working on her next manuscript with several other projects in the pipes.

When she's not writing, Aidan enjoys woodcarving, refinishing and refurbishing, playing the piano, and anything else she can do with her hands. She treasures her time with family and friends.

Aidan welcomes inquiry and feedback. Visit www.aidanis.com to keep up with Aidan's *Ransomed* blog, check out some of her artwork, find more information about her books, schedule Aidan to speak at your event, or contact this author directly.

# More from this Author

Games are not a new dynamic between man and God. From the first round of Hide and Seek in the Garden, we have been playing with Him. Thousands of years later, our game is the same. *Recess with Jesus* invites us to experience God's willingness to meet us here and play alongside us with a new strategy, a new set of rules, and a victory that maybe doesn't count for much on this playground but promises a greater prize.

This is not a book of answers. This is not a step-by-step guide to God and faith. This is not one of those books that asks us to step into David's or Martha's or Jonah's shoes and attempt to find their God just the way they experienced Him. God wants to meet us in our own shoes - or barefoot in the grass. He wants us to look around our playground and understand the offense of our defense of our games. We were never meant to play this way. We play to win, but for all our winning, we lose.

The familiarity of the playground opens us to a new way of looking at our relationship with Christ by starting at a place we all know, love, and fondly remember before pushing us deeper into discipleship. Each chapter is framed by Scripture and perfect for a quick read...but never a quick think. The powerful metaphor and thought-provoking twists of word in each familiar playground game catch us off-guard and stir us toward something more.

Who knew Four Square was a matter of the heart?

Made in the USA
Monee, IL
19 June 2023